NEOPLATONISM

IN RELATION TO

CHRISTIANITY

T0382418

NEOPLATONISM

IN RELATION TO

CHRISTIANITY

AN ESSAY

by

CHARLES ELSEE, M.A.

Sometime Scholar and Naden Divinity Student
of St John's College, Cambridge

CAMBRIDGE:
at the University Press
1908

CAMBRIDGE
UNIVERSITY PRESS

University Printing House, Cambridge CB2 8BS, United Kingdom

Published in the United States of America by Cambridge University Press, New York

Cambridge University Press is part of the University of Cambridge.

It furthers the University's mission by disseminating knowledge in the pursuit of
education, learning and research at the highest international levels of excellence.

www.cambridge.org
Information on this title: www.cambridge.org/9781107646025

© Cambridge University Press 1908

First published 1908
First paperback edition 2014

A catalogue record for this publication is available from the British Library

ISBN 978-1-107-64602-5 Paperback

PREFACE

THE following pages are the expansion of an essay which was awarded the Hulsean Prize in 1901, and they are now published in accordance with the terms of that bequest. In apologising for the long interval which has elapsed between the award of the prize and the publication of the essay, the author can only plead the pressure of other work, first at a College Mission in Walworth, and latterly at Leeds. At the same time this very delay has enabled him to grasp what a real bearing the speculations of the Neoplatonists, and their adaptations by the Christian Fathers, have upon much that is being said and written at the present day. Let the reader for instance compare what Plotinus or Augustine has to say on the subject of evil with the teaching of the "New Theology," and he will at once see how thoughts which are floating in men's minds to-day have been expressed with discrimination in the past. Or let him join the crowd that listens to the street-corner preacher of materialism, and then notice how 'Dionysius' deals with the question of finite man's comprehension of an infinite God. Truly, if we wish to see beyond the giants of the past, there is much to be said for climbing on their shoulders.

The subject of the essay is " Neoplatonism in relation to Christianity." The addition of this qualifying clause serves to limit the field of the enquiry, and to differentiate its object from that of a history of philosophy. The writer of such a history regards Neoplatonism purely from a philosophical standpoint. He draws out its relation to earlier and later systems, and seeks to assign to it its proper place in the development of human thought. Neoplatonism however was not merely a great philosophical revival : it was a part of a yet greater religious movement: and it is the latter aspect which this essay has to set forth.

For nearly two hundred years the Christian Church had been increasing, alike in numerical strength and in intellectual vigour, until it threatened not only to rival but absolutely to overpower the old pagan system of the Roman Empire. Persecution had been employed against it in vain. It gradually became obvious that if the new sect was to be exterminated, methods must be adopted far more vigorous and systematic than most of the Emperors were able or willing to employ, and the last and most statesmanlike of the persecutors endeavoured not so much to destroy Christianity, as to reduce it to its original position as a mean and vulgar superstition of the lower classes.

But direct persecution was not the only weapon which was levelled against the new religion. There were intervals of rest for the Church, during which the struggle was carried on in the form of literary controversy; and Neoplatonism was the greatest of these attempts to meet Christianity on its own ground, and by fair argument to show the superiority of the old paganism.

Accordingly the first chapter of this essay has been devoted to the discussion of the actual state of religion in the heathen world, at the commencement of the third century of the Christian era. The next two chapters deal with the relation of Neoplatonism to earlier systems of Greek speculation and with the first beginnings of Christian philosophy, whilst a fourth chapter has been given up to the general history of the school, together with the names of contemporary Christian writers. In the fifth chapter will be found a more detailed discussion of the mutual relations between Church and School, tracing their development from apparent alliance to bitter antagonism, and again, after this period of antagonism, to the gradual absorption of Neoplatonic principles by the Church.

C. E.

Clergy House, Leeds.
October 9, 1908.

CONTENTS

LIST OF MODERN WORKS CONSULTED

J. C. I. GIESELER, *Text-book of Ecclesiastical History*, 1836.

A. NEANDER, *History of Christian Religion*, trans. Torrey, 1850–58.

F. UEBERWEG, *History of Philosophy*, Eng. trans. 1872.

F. D. MAURICE, *Moral and Metaphysical Philosophy*, 1873.

A. HARNACK, *History of Dogma*, trans. Millar, 1897.

J. E. ERDMANN, *History of Philosophy*, trans. Hough, 1898.

J. B. CROZIER, *History of Intellectual Development*, 1897.

H. H. MILMAN, *History of Latin Christianity*, 4th Ed. 1883.

RITTER and PRELLER, *Historia Philosophiae Graecae*, ed. Wellman, 1898.

SMITH and WACE, *Dictionary of Christian Biography*, 1877–1887.

J. RÉVILLE, *La Religion à Rome sous les Sévères*, 1886.

E. HERRIOT, *Philon le Juif*, 1898.

J. DRUMMOND, *Philo Judaeus*, 1888.

E. DE FAYE, *Clément d'Alexandrie*, 1898.

T. WHITTAKER, *The Neoplatonists*, 1901.

T. TAYLOR, *Selected works of Plotinus, translated*, ed. Mead, 1895.

C. BIGG, *Christian Platonists of Alexandria*, 1886.

W. R. INGE, *Christian Mysticism*, 1899.

A. ZIMMERN, *Porphyry to Marcella*, 1896.

B. F. WESTCOTT, *Religious Thought in the West*, 1891.

G. H. RENDALL, *The Emperor Julian*, 1879.

A. GARDNER, *Synesius of Cyrene*, 1886.

J. C. NICOL, *Synesius of Cyrene, His Life and Writings*, 1887.

T. R. GLOVER, *Life and Letters in the Fourth Century*, 1901.

L. GRANDGEORGE, *St Augustin et le Néoplatonisme*, 1896.

E. W. WATSON, *Hilary of Poictiers* (Library of Nicene and Post-Nicene Fathers IX, 1899).

W. MOORE and H. A. WILSON, *Gregory of Nyssa* (Library of Nicene and Post-Nicene Fathers V, 1893).

H. F. STEWART, *Boethius*, 1891.

CHAPTER I

ROMAN RELIGION IN THE THIRD CENTURY

THE period in which Neoplatonism takes its rise is essentially an age of transition. Lying as it does between the age of pure Græco-Roman paganism and the final triumph of Christianity, it is the period in which both of the opposing forces are making their preparations for the last great struggle. Paganism arms itself with the new philosophy and summons to its aid all the forces of Roman conservatism; whilst Christianity, which has already in great measure secured its hold on the masses now attacks the highest circles of society, and endeavours to satisfy the craving for a true system of religious philosophy.

But before entering upon a detailed discussion of the religion of the Roman Empire in the third century[1], we may by way of introduction take a passing glance at the picture which Lucian gives of

---

[1] Throughout this chapter I have ventured for the sake of brevity to employ, without further qualification, the phrase "the third century." The period discussed would be more accurately described as the half century between the death of Commodus and the accession of Philippus Arabs; commencing with the accession of Septimius Severus in 193 A.D., and extending to the death of Gordianus Junior in the year 244.

Roman society and religion in the earlier part of the
second.   Shallow and heartless as he is, he nevertheless occupies a position of his own.   When considering
the evidence of the Christian apologists we are sometimes tempted to think that it must be prejudiced.
The writers are carrying on a controversy against a
system for which they feel that they have something
better to substitute, and whose weak points they are
bound, in spite of themselves, to exaggerate.   They
are liable to persecution, and therefore they may tend
to overestimate their own simple faith and purity in
contrast with the unbelief and licentiousness of the
pagan world around them.   But Lucian's position is
different.   He feels no fear of persecution.   He has
no special wish to regenerate or to reform mankind.
He is a satirist, who writes in order to amuse himself
by showing his utter contempt for the dead system
that claimed to be the religion of the Empire.

This contempt is of course most openly expressed
in such works as the *Juppiter Tragoedus* and the
Dialogues of the Gods.   But even if we leave these
satirical works on one side, we still find in Lucian the
clearest evidence of the low state into which religion
had fallen.   The memoir of *Alexander the False
Prophet* and the account of the *Death of Peregrinus*
are documents of considerable historical value ; and
in these we see, on the one hand the love of notoriety
for which Peregrinus is ready to pay the price even
of self-immolation ; and, on the other, the blind
credulity on which Alexander is able to work by the
crudest of methods—a credulity which is not limited
to the ignorant peasants of Asia Minor, but extends

to the highest circles of Roman society. And in both works alike we see the love of sensation which has taken the place of the old Roman reverence for religion.

It is a matter for regret that Lucian has not given us a more complete account of the Christians of his day. The Church was passing through a great crisis: she had to face the question whether she was to remain a small society of religious devotees, or to go forward and take her place at the head of the great religions of the world. The Montanists preferred to remain where they were: the Church as a whole decided to go forward. At such a time the evidence of a writer like Lucian would have been of peculiar interest. But he passes over Christianity almost in silence. In his authentic works there are perhaps not more than two direct references to it. He tells us[1] that Alexander was wont, at the commencement of his "Mysteries" to cry "If any Atheist or Christian or Epicurean have come to spy upon the Ceremonies, let him flee." And it is to be remembered that Alexander would be no mean judge of the audience best suited for his purpose, so that his warning cry suggests that the Christians at this time were not all such simple and credulous folk as we are sometimes inclined to suppose. The other reference to Christianity occurs in the account of Peregrinus[2]. In his younger days this person had professed himself a Christian, and Lucian describes with mingled admiration and contempt the way in which his fellow-Christians tended him during an imprisonment for

[1] Lucian, *Alex.* 38.   [2] Lucian, *De Morte Peregrini*, 12.

the sake of the faith.   This is the passage that gives
us the clearest view of Lucian's own ideas upon the
subject of Christianity.   It is too much to say with
Suidas that he is a blasphemer ; for that charge can
only be made good by reference to the pseudo-
Lucianic *Philopatris*.   In the account of Peregrinus[1],
the reference to "their crucified sophist" expresses
rather pity for Christian credulity than downright
contempt.

Such are the only direct references to Christianity
which are to be found in Lucian's writings.   It is
clear that the subject had but little interest for him.
It failed to excite his curiosity, and he practically
ignores it.

With regard however to the condition of pagan
thought in his day, Lucian is a most valuable witness.
He is a man of considerable ability, at once thoroughly
versatile and thoroughly sceptical, whilst his detached
attitude lends especial weight to his opinions.   The
impression that we gain from a study of his writings
is that there was no central force in paganism at this
time : the old powers were found to be effete, or, at
the best, to be spasmodic and local in their effects,
and it seemed as though the whole system were
crumbling away through sheer inability to survive.

But it must not be assumed that this would be
equally true as a description of the religion of the
Empire half a century later.   In the period between
Lucian and Plotinus there occurred an extraordinary
revival or recrudescence of paganism.   This was not
merely a revival of external ceremonial, such as took

[1] *Ib.* 13.

place in the time of Augustus. It was a genuine refor-
mation, and it led to the growth of a more spiritual
religion than the Roman world had ever known.

Of this revival of paganism no contemporary
historian has left us a complete account. Indirect
evidence however is not wanting. It is to be derived
in abundance from sources at once numerous and
varied. Much can be gathered from heathen writers,
—from historians like Dio Cassius and Lampridius,
from philosophers like Porphyry, and from sophists like
Philostratus. Further contributions may be levied
from Christian writers, from Clement of Alexandria
and Origen, from Tertullian and Augustine. Nor
must the evidence of inscriptions be neglected, which
is invaluable, in this as in other cases, as affording
contemporary corroboration to the statements of our
other authorities.

The characteristic note of Roman society at this
period was its cosmopolitanism. More than one generation had passed away since Juvenal uttered his
lament[1] that the Orontes was emptying itself into
the Tiber, and no attempt had been made to check
the stream of foreign immigration. The aristocracy
of the second century, liberal and progressive as it
had been in matters of legislation, had been comparatively conservative in matters of religion. But
the end of that century witnessed a change. The
religious revival of this period affected all classes of
pagan society, and the enthusiasm which it aroused
was expended as much in the welcoming of new
divinities as in the service of the old ones.

[1] Juv. 3. 62.

The mere number of gods and goddesses who succeeded in obtaining recognition in the Empire at this time is astounding. It is impossible within the limits of the present chapter to do more than mention the principal classes into which they fall, and to touch upon one or two of the most important of the deities. The old Roman gods were still the official guardians of the state[1]. Their temples continued to stand in unimpaired splendour; they themselves still received sacrifices on all important occasions; and the office of Pontifex Maximus was still conferred upon each successive Emperor. The old colleges of priests, augurs, and the like, still existed, and membership in them was an honour that was much sought after; whilst the various guilds and societies for purposes of trade or of mutual benefit all had their religious aspects.

Of the cults which became prevalent after the fall of the Republic, the most widespread was the worship of the Emperor[2]. As a general rule the Romans did not attempt to impose the worship of their gods upon conquered peoples, but in this particular case they made an exception. The worship of the Emperor was enforced in order to add to the stability of the Empire, by causing men's religious emotions to be centred on the man in whom the executive power was vested, and thus to efface those rivalries between the various towns and tribes which tended to foster a local and national rather than an imperial patriotism. As each town was merged in the vast Empire, the

---

[1] J. Réville, *La Réligion à Rome sous les Sévères*, p. 26.
[2] Réville, p. 30.

importance of local politics and local religion tended
to decline, and the place of the local deity was taken
by the Genius of the Empire, worshipped in concrete
form in the person of the Emperor.

To the student of Church History this cult is of
the greatest importance.   Its enforced observance
formed, in times of persecution, the dividing line
between Christian and Pagan, and refusal to sacrifice
to the Emperor was regarded as a species of treason.
For the purposes of this essay its chief importance
lies in the fact that it is one of the signs that the
general drift of paganism tended towards some form
of monotheism.   The office, rather than the person
of the reigning Emperor, was the real object of
worship : and the many inscriptions extant in honour
of the Wisdom, Justice or Clemency of the Emperor
show how completely he had come to be regarded
as a secondary providence, visible, accessible, and on
earth ; a divinity so near at hand that, according to
Tertullian[1], men were more ready to perjure themselves by all the gods than by the Genius of the
Emperor.   At the same time, the apotheosis of
departed Emperors did not tend to raise the tone of
heathenism.   Rather it served to diminish the value
of deity and to place an efficient weapon in the hands
of those who wished to bring discredit upon paganism.

The reigning Emperor was usually worshipped,
not in person, but through the medium of his *Genius*[2].
But the possession of a Genius was not the prerogative
of the Emperor alone.   There was a special Genius
for every man, every family, every nation ; we even

[1] Tert. *Apol.* 28.   [2] Réville, p. 39.

find them assigned to the gods. Their worship was a
survival from the primitive Roman religion which
recognised a special deity for every single department
of life: but the current ideas about the precise nature
of Genii had been considerably modified by the
Greek notions about *daemons*, and it would seem that
in the third century there was a considerable variety
in the opinions prevalent upon the subject. They
were regarded, sometimes as immanent in the persons
or things to which they were attached, sometimes as
entirely external: some Genii were almost on a level
with the gods, others again were but little higher in
the scale of being than their charges. The Genius of
each individual corresponds closely to the Christian
conception of a guardian angel; as compared with
the gods he resembles the family doctor, who watches
over the wellbeing of his charges on all ordinary occasions, whilst they are the specialists, one or another of
whom is summoned in cases of emergency.

Similar to the Genii were a number of personifications of abstract qualities to whom worship was
offered. Such were *Honos*, *Spes*, *Libertas*, *Virtus*:
the object worshipped being in each case the Genius
of the quality named. How far these were mere
abstractions, and to what extent they were regarded
as actual deities, the worshipper himself would probably have found it hard to explain.

The belief in Genii was not merely a vulgar
superstition. The philosophers recognised a world of
spirits intermediate between gods and men: beings
whom Celsus describes[1] as the proconsuls or satraps

[1] Cf. Orig. *c. Cels.* 8. 35.

of the gods, and whom Plotinus defines[1] as eternal
like the gods, but participating in the material world
like men.   There is also, in the writings of the
Christian Fathers, ample evidence of a firm belief in
angelic powers : and, more than this, the Fathers do
not throw any doubt upon either the existence or the
potency of the spirits worshipped by the pagans[2].
They differ from heathen writers only in maintaining
that these particular spirits are invariably evil.

The foregoing deities, however orientalised their
worship may have become, were at least Roman in
origin.   But the greater part of the conglomeration
of creeds, which formed the religion of the Empire,
was derived from foreign sources[3].   Egypt and
Carthage, Phrygia and Syria, all sent their respective
contingents to the Roman pantheon : even the wild
German tribes were not unrepresented.   It was the
necessary result of the mixed character of the
population.   Eastern slaves carried with them superstitions from the East : merchants of Alexandria
brought with them Egyptian gods as well as their
wares ; above all, the soldiers, recruited mainly from
the frontiers of the Empire, carried their own deities
and their own forms of worship wherever they went.
Sooner or later the strange gods drifted to Rome,
and, once planted, their worship was bound to spread.
The mere novelty of these foreign cults made them
objects of curiosity : the penal enactments, which
still existed though never enforced, against those who
encouraged strange rites, may have served to give

[1] Plot. *Enn.* 3. 5, 6.   [2] Cf. Tert. *Apol.* 22.
[3] Réville, p. 47.

them the added attractiveness of forbidden fruit; whilst they received a further impetus from the fact that many of them possessed special orders of priests whose sole business lay in the propagation of their religion. But the true cause of their success lay in the inability of the old Roman religion to satisfy the spiritual longings of the people. The old worship had served so long as Rome was struggling for bare existence; but even before the beginning of the Empire there were signs of the prevalence of a profound sense of religious discontent. Something less barren, less utterly unspiritual, was required, and any cult that claimed to supply this need was sure to be welcomed.

Foremost among the Eastern divinities, which came crowding into all parts of the Empire, stands the Egyptian Isis. Temples and statues without number were erected in her honour: the Emperors themselves took part in her processions. She was originally the personification of the female element in nature, but as time went on she assumed the attributes of several Greek and Roman goddesses— Juno, Ceres, Proserpine and Venus—and became moreover the patroness of shipping and commerce. She possessed not only an elaborate priesthood, but a lower order of mendicant brethren; and the magnificent ritual in her temples, alike in the daily worship and on the occasion of great festivals, cannot but have had its effect on the popular mind.

The other chief Egyptian deities were Osiris, the dog-headed Anubis, and Serapis, who afterwards gained greater popularity even than Isis. In the time of the Syrian Emperors, and in particular under Septimius Severus, Caracalla, and Alexander Severus, these Egyptian divinities were in high favour.

It is impossible here to discuss in detail the systems that were introduced from Phrygia, Syria and Phoenicia. There was a certain similarity, alike in organization and in ritual, between all these Eastern religions. They usually had an order of priests : often also an order of mendicant friars, whose sole claim to sanctity seems, in some cases, to have consisted in their profession of poverty. Their ritual was characterized by the prevalence of " mysteries " and by elaborate ceremonial, every detail of which had its allegorical meaning. But they drew their supporters from a lower stratum of society than that with which we are concerned. They could not claim the immemorial antiquity of the Egyptian cults, and there was moreover about them a certain lack of refinement, which could not but be distasteful to the philosophical mind. They were tolerated, as meeting the religious needs of those to whom they appealed ; but they failed to secure the respect and adherence of men of culture.

There remains however one deity who must not be passed over[1]. This is Mithras, the one Persian divinity who acquired a hold on the Roman Empire. We first hear of his being brought to Rome in connexion with Pompey's suppression of the Cilician pirates[2]; but his worship attracted but little attention in the West until the middle of the second century of the Christian era. Then the Oriental tendency,

---

[1] Réville, p. 77.   [2] 67 B.C. Cf. Plutarch, *Pomp.* 24.

discernible at Rome under the Antonines, brought him into favour : Antoninus Pius built a temple in his honour at Ostia, and Marcus Aurelius built another on the Vatican. At this period he is mentioned, with disdain it is true, but none the less with obvious apprehension in Lucian's *Council of the Gods*[1]. Under the Severi his popularity grew by leaps and bounds, and it looked as though in another generation he would reign supreme.

To the Roman, Mithras was essentially the Sun-god of purity and power, able and willing to protect his worshippers in this world and the next. He was regarded as the creator of the world, the deliverer from cold and darkness. To many of his worshippers the moral and mystical teaching was of far greater importance than the doctrine of Mithras as the ruler of the physical world. His mysteries dealt probably for the most part with the future destiny of the soul, of which he is regarded as the saviour and regenerator. In the Mithraic catacomb on the Appian Way[2] the course of the soul after death is described : we see it escorted by Mercury before Pluto and Proserpine, in the presence of the Fates, and finally conducted to the banquet of the just.

Mithras-worship has been described as the pagan form of Gnosticism[3]. In both alike may be traced the love of mystical speculation; the growth of the idea of redemption; the belief that proper ritual could atone for a life of evil. It is interesting to notice that a worshipper could make atonement

[1] *Deor. Conc.* 9.   [2] Réville, p. 94.
[3] Réville, p. 93.

without himself undergoing the strain and discomfort
of the ritual. For instance, the most striking of all
the rites of Mithras was the *Taurobolium,* or baptism
of blood[1]. This ceremony, whereby the worshipper
was drenched with the warm blood that flowed from
the victim's throat, was supposed to bring certain
regeneration. And it is to be remarked that it could
be performed on a priest for the benefit of some other
person. The stress was laid on the *opus operatum* of
the magical sacrament, not on the bodily presence of
the individual for whose benefit it was offered.

We cannot here discuss the relation of Mithras-
worship to Christianity. The early Christians were
well aware of the similarity between the rites of
Mithras and those of the Church. Actual connexion
however there appears not to have been, though
Justin Martyr[2] and Tertullian[3] denounce the washing
of neophytes, the confirmation of the initiated, and
the consecration of bread and water, as diabolical
parodies of Christian sacraments.

The worship of Mithras spread rapidly, and at one
time bid fair to become the final religion of the
Empire. The high morality that it inculcated, and
the almost military discipline that it maintained in
its vast body of devotees seemed to give a promise
of permanence which the other pagan systems could
not offer. But it was not to be. After the time of
Julian, Christianity took its place as the dominant
religion of the West; and in later days Mahom-
medanism drove out Mithras-worship from its last
strongholds in the Eastern Empire.

[1] Réville, p. 96.   [2] *Apol.* I. 66.   [3] *De Praescr.* 40.

Such are a few of the main types of religion prevalent in the Roman Empire during the third century. No attempt has been made to give a complete catalogue of the gods who received worship at this period : whole classes have been omitted altogether, and no class has been described in its entirety. But the sketch, fragmentary as it is, may help to make clear the kind of religion which many of the Neoplatonists felt themselves called upon to defend. Its most striking characteristic is perhaps toleration. Never in the history of Western civilisation have so many deities been recognised at the same time. And, paradoxical as it may appear, the general result of this excessive polytheism was to cause a strong current of feeling towards monotheism. Each deity was regarded as one particular form of "the Divine," and this idea received confirmation from the partial identity of the symbols and attributes ascribed to different gods.

This is the method by which the philosophers reconcile themselves to polytheism. "There is one sun and one sky over all nations" says Plutarch[1], "and one deity under many names." Even Celsus recognises one deity alone, but he recommends every nation to maintain its own cults, and so to honour the sovereign by showing respect to his representative. The personality of the various gods is thus more or less passed over. They are, in fact, gods from the point of view of religion, abstractions from that of philosophy. And a judicious use of the allegorical method of interpretation made it a comparatively

[1] *De Isid. et Osir.* 67.

simple matter to reconcile monotheism in theory with polytheism in practice. It may be well to add a few words with regard to what has been said about the attitude of the philosophers, and in particular, of the Neoplatonists, towards pagan polytheism. It is true that the philosopher, strictly speaking, has nothing to do with systems of religion. His speculations may take a theological form, and he may even lay down general principles as to the means whereby man may hope to live in harmony with the Deity: but with the outward forms of religion he has no connexion. Moreover, in considering the Neoplatonists we are tempted to imagine that the whole school shared the lofty position of Plotinus, and to forget that, until after the time of Julian, no other Neoplatonic writer confined himself to the discussion of abstract philosophy, or failed to make it clear that he wished definitely to support the pagan system. How far Plotinus had in view the defence of paganism, is a question which will be discussed later: at all events his contemporaries and his immediate followers were all tinged with Neopythagoreanism, and hardly deserve, in its highest sense, the title of Philosophers. They professed to be rationalists who by specious explanation could justify the existence of superstitious observances, but the true state of the case would seem rather to be that they were carried away by the spirit of the age, and used their rationalism to condone their own superstition.

The great defect in the religious revival of the third century was its utter lack of the spirit of criticism[1].

[1] Réville, p. 130.

It is true that this uncritical spirit was not limited to
that particular age, nor was it found among the
heathen alone. Thus Tacitus[1] among men of an
earlier generation, and Clement of Rome[2] and
Tertullian[3] among the Christians, were as ready to
accept the legend of the Phoenix as Celsus[4] or
Philostratus[5]. But in the third century the tide of ill-
regulated religious feeling produced a flood of superstition against which men of the keenest intellect
found it well nigh impossible to stand. It is hard, on
any other supposition, to explain how so many of
the great Neoplatonists could become upholders of
astrology and magic, and declare that these things
had a scientific basis in the influence of the stars and
the mutual relations of the elements.

The whole machinery of augury, prophecy, oracles
and the like was once again called into play, and all
classes of society had recourse to one or other of
these sources for aid and information upon every
conceivable subject. But the most important of these
means of communication with the unseen world were
the various " Mysteries." The existence of such rites
was not a new thing. The Eleusinian Mysteries had
already been long established in the days of Plato,
and the mysteries of the third century belong to the
same general type. The number of deities however
in whose honour they were celebrated, the high value
set upon initiation, and the crowds of persons who
were initiated, often into the mysteries of more than

[1] *Ann.* 6. 28.   [2] *Ep.* 1. 25.
[3] *De Res. Carn.* 13.   [4] Or. *c. Cels.* 4. 98.
[5] *Vit. Apoll.* 3. 49.

one deity, far surpassed anything that had been known
before.

There is in fact a fundamental difference between
the early Roman conception of religion and that of
the period with which we are now concerned[1]. The
old Roman religion was barren and cold. The stress
was laid on formal observances, the whole matter
being neither more nor less than a bargain. In return
for the proper sacrifices paid at the proper time and
in the proper manner the gods were expected to send
certain advantages to the worshipper. But by the
beginning of the third century there had sprung up a
real love for the gods, and a desire for communion
with them. The belief also in a future life was far
more definite than it had been in the Classical period.
The philosophers on the one hand, and the hierophants
of the various mysteries on the other, endeavoured to
set men's minds at rest upon this matter, and both
alike commanded the attention of those whom they
addressed. There arose moreover an idea of holiness
which had been practically unknown before[2]; and
with it an idea not unlike the Christian conception of
sin. It is not the same, for there is no notion of
man's voluntary deviation from the will of God.
But there is the longing for the attainment of a state
of purity, whether by a life of asceticism or by a
series of purifying ceremonies.

One other question remains to be discussed.
What was the attitude of the paganism of this period
towards Christianity? Toleration has already been
mentioned as the leading characteristic of the age,

[1] Réville, p. 143.   [2] Réville, p. 152.

and it is in consequence not surprising to find that, under the Syrian Emperors, the Church was more free from persecution than at any other time between the reigns of Nero and Constantine. But it was difficult to extend toleration to a religion that was itself intolerant; and, side by side with the readiness to abstain from persecution, there are here and there traces of an almost pathetic anxiety that the Christians should do their share, and acknowledge that the older religions, if not actually superior, were at least on the same level as their own, and worthy of the fullest re-cognition as partial manifestations of the same deity.

The attitude however of the Church was not conciliatory. Never perhaps has there been a writer so uncompromising as Tertullian, and even if, a generation later, Origen appears to be in sympathy with much of heathen philosophy, there is no question as to his position with regard to heathen religion. Accordingly attempts were made to weld the pagan systems into a single weapon, which could be used with effect against the new religion.

The first of these attempts was made during the supremacy of Julia Domna[1]. During the reigns of her husband, Septimius Severus, and of his successor Caracalla, this remarkable woman exercised an influence that was considerable even in matters of politics, whilst in the realm of art and literature her power was unquestioned. She gathered around her a literary circle of the best intellects of the age, recruited from all parts of the Empire, but principally from Greece and her native Syria. The tone of her

[1] Réville, p. 190.

coterie seems to have been brilliant and witty rather than scholarly ; the members were men of the type that feeds on the love of the marvellous, but they were deficient in the patience needful for deep thought, and they lacked the courage fully to face the real problems of life.   Their philosophy was Neopythagorean, their religion vague and comprehensive.   They hated irreligion, and loved variety, and they were moreover capable of professing doctrines of high purity whilst leading a life of considerable self-indulgence.

Their great contribution to the defence of paganism was the life of Apollonius of Tyana, which was composed at the suggestion of the Empress, written in the first instance by Damis, and afterwards re-written and transformed by Philostratus.   The subject of this biography was a real man, who lived at about the date to which he is here assigned, and in whose life occurred many of the principal episodes here described.   But the whole has been so interwoven with legend and fiction that it is well nigh impossible to disentangle the true from the false.   The philosopher of Tyana is in fact transformed into the patron saint, as it were, of third-century paganism, and the picture presented to us does not so much represent what Apollonius actually was, as what Philostratus would have liked him to be.

On the precise relation between the work of Philostratus and the Christian Gospels something will be said later : for the present it is sufficient to observe that the life and character of Apollonius, as here described, so far expressed the ideals of the age for which the book was written, that from being considered a mere provincial magician or charlatan,

Apollonius suddenly came to be revered by the whole
of pagan society as one who stood on a level with the
noblest spirits of the ancient world.   Caracalla[1] built
a temple in his honour : Alexander Severus[2] assigned
him a niche in his private chapel, side by side with
Orpheus and Alexander the Great; and later still
Eunapius[3] revered him as something more than man.
He is more than the prophet of paganism : he is the
incarnation of its highest hopes and aims.

But, as time went on, it became clear that the
effort had failed.   The composite picture of Alexander
constructed by the sophists of the third century was
no more able to hold its own against the Christ of the
Gospels than the disjointed forces of paganism to
prevail against the united strength of the organized
Church, and the heathen revival served only to pave
the way for the coming of the new religion which its
promoters were endeavouring to check.

Two other attempts may be mentioned, both of
which illustrate the desire for recognition from the
Christians to which allusion has already been made.
The first of these need not long detain us[4]: it was
thoroughly distasteful to many of the people, and its
chief interest lies in the indication which it gives of
the trend of pagan thought towards monotheism.
The Emperor Elagabalus was taken from the temple
at Emesa to be placed on the throne against his will.
He evinced no care whatever for the concerns of the
Empire except in the sphere of religion, and here his
sole object was the glorification of the god of Emesa.
He endeavoured to make the worship of this deity

---

[1] Dio Cass. 77. 18.   [2] Lamprid. *Alex. Sev.* 29.
[3] Eun. *Vit. Phil. Proem.* p. 3.   Boiss.   [4] Réville, p. 237.

the one religion of the Empire, by associating with
El-Gabal the symbols and functions of all the other
gods, and he expressed a hope that even Jews and
Christians might be persuaded to worship the supreme
God in the temple of El-Gabal. But his avowed
contempt for all things Roman made his action odious
to the upper classes : it never really affected the mass
of the people, and its effects disappeared immediately
after his death.

Elagabalus was succeeded by his cousin Alexander Severus, a man of very different type, whose
natural temperament and education alike tended to
give him the fullest sympathy with the old Roman
spirit. He enjoyed intellectual society and showed
the greatest reverence for the old gods, paying weekly
visits to the temples on the Capitol. In his own
private chapel he worshipped a curious assemblage of
famous men. The niches were filled with statues of
Apollonius, Christ, Abraham, Orpheus and Alexander
the Great[1]; whilst a lower order of heroes was also
represented which included the names of Vergil
and Cicero[2]. Alexander clearly hoped to solve the
problem of paganism by a religious eclecticism ;
calling into existence a hierarchy of the saints of all
the religions with which he was acquainted. He is
perhaps the noblest instance of the wide tolerance
towards which the comprehensive religion of his time
tended, but there was a certain lack of cohesion about
his schemes, alike in religion and politics, which prevented them from exercising any lasting influence.

---

[1] Lamprid. *Alex. Sev.* 29.   [2] *Ib.* 31.

CHAPTER II

EARLIER SYSTEMS OF GREEK PHILOSOPHY

IT will be well in the present chapter to describe the general state of philosophy in the period immediately preceding the rise of Neoplatonism, and to point out the earlier sources from which many of the Neoplatonic doctrines were derived. In order to secure these two objects it will be best, first to give a short account of the various stages of Greek philosophy with which we are here concerned, marking the appearance of each distinctive point of teaching as it arises, and then to take a rapid survey of the general condition of philosophy in the early years of the third century. No attempt however will be made to give an exhaustive catalogue of all the great philosophers or even of all the various schools, for such a list would seem to lie outside the province of the present essay.

The first school of Greek philosophy occupied itself with speculations upon the origin and constitution of the physical world. This primitive Ionian school, instituted by Thales far back in the seventh century, continued to exist until late in the fifth

century before Christ.   The majority of its members
need not detain us.   Their aim was to discover the
material out of which the physical world was
fashioned, a material which the earlier members of
the school sought in a single primary substance, the
later ones in a number of different elements.   At the
same time there may here and there be traced signs
of the beginnings of something more than merely
physical speculation.   Thus Heraclitus of Ephesus, in
addition to his famous aphorism on the universal
prevalence of constant change[1], also propounded some
sort of teaching on the subject of a *Logos*[2].   Heraclitus
recognised no transcendent deity, so that his Logos
must not be in any way associated with the Jewish
conception of the " Word of God[3]."   It is eternal and
self-subsisting, and seems to represent the " rational
self-evolution of the world," the law of progress by
means of constant strife[4].   The name λόγος was
apparently selected, as being less encumbered with
human and material associations than either νοῦς or
φρήν[5].

We seem here to have the first beginning of the
conception of an universal Reason which occupies so
prominent a position in later philosophy.   There is
not sufficient evidence to make clear the details of
Heraclitus' teaching:—whether for instance the Logos
was possessed of consciousness, and again whether it
was identical with the fire which Heraclitus declared
to be the primary substance.   It is perhaps most

[1] Heracl. *frag.* 41 ; Ritter and Preller, p. 27.
[2] *Frag.* 2; R. P. p. 26.
[3] Cf. Drummond, *Philo Judaeus* I. pp. 34, 46.
[4] Heracl. *frag.* 46; R. P. p. 27.   [5] Drummond I. p. 47.

probable that the system of Heraclitus was a refined
form of pantheism[1], and that his Logos was not
possessed of the consciousness which Plotinus claimed
for his Mind ($\nu o\hat{v}\varsigma$); but it is impossible to speak with
certainty.

Heraclitus is said to have flourished about the
year 500 B.C., and the same date is assigned to the
birth of the only other member of the Ionian school
to whom it is necessary to refer. This was Anaxagoras
of Clazomenae, whose doctrine of the universal Mind
($\nu o\hat{v}\varsigma$) so completely overshadowed the speculations
of Heraclitus upon the Logos, that this use of the
term Logos almost disappeared from Greek philosophy, until it was revived five centuries later by
Philo.

This universal Mind of Anaxagoras, whether
strictly immaterial or composed of the subtlest form
of matter, is clearly distinguished from the rest of the
universe. It is conceived as infinite and self-subsisting,
free alike from external mixture and external control[2].
It possesses universal knowledge and pervades and
governs all things that have soul. In the original
foundation of the world it plays a smaller part than
might have been expected, appearing only as giving
rise to the first revolution which produced the combination of objects as they are now known to us; but,
in the organic world, it is the vital principle, in which
plants as well as animals have a share.

The sixth century before Christ witnessed the rise
of two other schools of Greek philosophy, both of

---

[1] Cf. Drummond I. p. 44.
[2] Anax. apud Simplic. *Phys.* 156. 13; R. P. p. 117.

which left their mark upon the system with which we are concerned. The first of these schools was founded by Pythagoras[1], who laid stress upon the influence of Number, and who was perhaps the earliest Greek exponent of the doctrine of transmigration of souls. The mystical form of his teaching had a great attraction for the philosophers who immediately precede the rise of the Neoplatonists and although there are few traces of his influence in the writings of Plotinus, yet the lives of Pythagoras composed by Porphyry and Iamblichus, and the abundant references to him in their other writings, are sufficient evidence of the esteem in which he was held by the later Neoplatonists.

The other school of pre-Socratic philosophy to which reference has been made is that of the Eleatics. Its principal members were Xenophanes, Parmenides, Zeno, and Melissus; and their chief contribution to philosophy consisted in speculations upon the nature of Being. They were impressed with the inability of the human mind adequately to grasp the true nature of the deity. The protest of Xenophanes against anthropomorphic conceptions[2] of the gods need not detain us, but a few words may be said with regard to the positive teaching of the school. In their view the essence of Being consists in unity and immutability, and its attributes are described by a series of paradoxes. It is at once neither finite nor infinite, neither movable nor immovable; it had no beginning and it will have no end[3]. In addition to this doctrine of

---

[1] Cf. Ueberweg, pp. 42—49.   [2] Xenophanes, *frag.* 6; R. P. p. 79.
[3] *De Melisso*, 977 b; R. P. p. 85.

Being, the Eleatics also asserted what may perhaps
best be called the positive non-existence of Non-
Being[1], the dark principle which lies at the root of all
the changing phenomena of the world in which we
live.

There are but few direct references to the Eleatic
school in the writings of the Neoplatonists, though
Plotinus twice mentions Parmenides with respect[2],
but the indirect influence which they exerted was
very considerable. If it is in the writings of Heraclitus
and Anaxagoras that we have to look for the first
speculations upon Mind, it is in those of the Eleatics
that we find the germ of Plotinus' teaching about
" The Good."

The next name that arrests our attention is that
of Socrates. Of the vast influence exercised by this
philosopher over the whole of subsequent Greek
thought there can be no doubt, but it was an influence
due rather to the methods which he employed than
to the actual details of his teaching. Like Ammonius
Saccas the founder of the Neoplatonic school, Socrates
was not a writer ; and it is moreover necessary to
distinguish his authentic teaching from that which is
merely put in his mouth by Plato. In Xenophon's
Memorabilia however we are fortunate enough to
possess materials which are free from Platonic
influence, and from a comparison of the two portraits
the following particulars may be gleaned. Socrates
appears to have been the first thinker to introduce the
doctrine of a divine purpose in creation[3]. The world

[1] Cf. Plat. *Soph.* 237a; R. P. p. 90.
[2] Plot. *Enn.* 5. 1. 8, 6. 6. 18.   [3] Drummond I. p. 52 ff.

has been designed by the gods for the use of man, to whose needs many ordinances are clearly subservient[1]. Thus man derives advantage from the alternation of day and night, from the existence of the lower animals and of fire; whilst the gods' special care for him is manifest in the gifts of human intellect and ingenuity, as well as in the provision of oracles for his guidance. The precise relation between the divine and the human is less clearly expressed. The human soul is said to partake of the divine nature, as the body partakes of the physical elements[2]. But Socrates is here involved in the difficulty which Anaxagoras had felt before him[3]. He regards the deity as personal—believing perhaps in one supreme God with a number of inferior and local deities beneath him—and at the same time he holds that man's soul is a part of God. To this problem he has no satisfactory answer to give; but the perception of the difficulty is the first step towards its solution, and the participation of man in the divine nature explains and justifies his endeavour to know God.

From Socrates we pass on to his great disciple whose philosophy Plotinus and his school professed to revive and develope. The great addition made by Plato to Greek speculation was his doctrine of Ideas. These are to us only abstract notions, and yet they are eternal realities. They are, as it were, the Genii of the various general notions, exempt from all space limitations, but capable of motion, possessed of life and intelligence, belonging to a world of real being[4].

---

[1] Xen. *Mem.* 4. 3. 3—10.　　　　[2] *Ib.* 4. 3. 14.
[3] Drummond I. p. 56.　　[4] Plato, *Soph.* 248 E; R. P. p. 243.

The Ideas are not all on the same level: there are various ranks to be distinguished among them, and the highest of all is the Idea of "The Good[1]."

The universe in which we live falls short of the perfection of the world of Ideas. It has been created by the good God in order to express his goodness; but fashioned as it is out of indeterminate matter (τὸ ἄπειρον), it does not entirely or adequately fulfil that purpose. There cannot however be more than one such universe, for this one, despite its imperfections, is the best that can be made. It is pervaded by a Soul and is, in fact, a rational being[2].

Now the creator is incapable of making anything that is imperfect. He therefore creates the lesser deities and points out to them the need of mortal creatures[3]. They then proceed to create the bodies, whilst he creates the souls, one for each star, ready to be assigned to mortal bodies as need arises. The soul therefore is divine in origin and in nature: it exists before the body as well as after it. Like the soul of the universe, the soul of the individual forms a link between the world of phenomena and the Ideas, and even while in the body it has from time to time flashes of recollection of its former life in the higher sphere. In the tenth book of the *Republic*[4] there is to be found a doctrine of transmigration of souls; but it is not clear how far this is to be taken seriously, and how far it is only a picturesque addition to the myth in which it occurs.

---

[1] Plato, *Rep.* VI. 508 C; R. P. p. 251.

[2] Plato, *Tim.* 29 D; R. P. p. 257.

[3] Plato, *Tim.* 41 D. Drummond I. p. 66.   [4] *Rep.* X. 617 E.

The schools which professed to be the guardians
of Plato's philosophy, and which are known as the
Old, Middle, and New Academy, need not detain us[1].
They do not in any real sense bridge the gulf between
Plato and Plotinus, nor are there many references
to them in the writings of the Neoplatonists. Their
doctrines are often directly opposed to those of the
Neoplatonists, or deal with entirely different subjects.
Thus in the Old Academy Speusippus[2] taught that
"The Best," although the first in rank, is the last of
the Ideas in order of development, a doctrine which
Plotinus would never have accepted; whilst Heraclides
devoted himself to astronomy. Xenocrates[3] is said
to have connected the Ideas with numbers, thereby
showing a tendency towards Pythagoreanism such as is
also noticeable in the Neoplatonist Iamblichus. The
Middle Academy, alike in its early period under
Arcesilas and in its later one under Carneades, was
almost entirely sceptical in its views; but in the New
Academy there was a return to more dogmatic
teaching, and Antiochus of Ascalon made an attempt
to combine the teaching of Plato with certain
Aristotelian and Stoic doctrines, which resembles the
eclectic syncretism of the Neoplatonists[4].

Of the vast system of Aristotle it is impossible
here to give a detailed account[5]. His work was
essentially that of a systematizer. He took the great
principles of Plato and endeavoured to show how

[1] See Ueberweg, pp. 133—136.
[2] Arist. *Met.* XII. 7; R. P. p. 280.
[3] Stobaeus, *Ecl.* I. 62; R. P. p. 282.
[4] Sext. *Pyrrh.* I. 235; R. P. p. 447.
[5] Cf. Crozier, vol. I. p. 54 ff.

they could be made to explain the phenomena of the world around us. In order to do this it was necessary to define clearly the mutual relations of the Platonic elements, which Aristotle accordingly considered in two groups. In the first group he placed "The Good," together with the Ideas, which he regarded as being contained within the mind of The Good, and not, as Plato had held, as having an independent existence. In the second group he placed indeterminate matter (τὸ ἄπειρον), and with it the same Ideas as have been already mentioned in the first group. The next step was to find the means whereby the lifeless mixture of Ideas and Matter should become instinct with life, and this he found in Motion, derived from the Ether that fills the vault of heaven, whose revolutions enable the Ideas to unite with the formless matter, and thereby cause the world to come into being[1].

The position of matter in the system of Aristotle is thus different from that which it occupies in the writings of Plato. It is no longer a purely negative principle, but capable of direct union with the Ideas. In this particular case, Plotinus was led by the Oriental tendencies of his age to follow Plato, and indeed to go beyond Plato in his abhorrence of things material, but in other respects the teaching of Aristotle had a very real bearing upon the Neoplatonic system. The incident mentioned by Porphyry[2] of Plotinus' bidding Amelius to reply to Porphyry's pamphlet on the theme "That things intelligible have their subsistence outside Intelligence" shows that in

---

[1] Arist. *De Caelo* I. 3. 270A; R. P. p. 329.
[2] *Vit. Plot.* 18.

this instance, where Porphyry, and in all probability
his teacher Longinus, followed Plato, Plotinus had
adopted an Aristotelian attitude: and, in the writings
of the later Neoplatonists, commentaries upon the
works of Aristotle and treatises upon his relation to
Plato are of frequent occurrence.

The tendency of Greek philosophy after the time
of Aristotle was to become practical rather than
speculative. The subjects with which the Stoics and
Epicureans occupied themselves were the relations of
philosophy to religion, and above all the quest of that
indifference to things external which alone could arm
the individual with calmness and fortitude under all
circumstances. The Epicureans we may pass over.
Beyond accepting in its entirety the atomic theory of
Democritus, they made no attempt to discover the
final cause of the creation and government of the
world; and they exercised no influence on the later
systems with which we are concerned. Even the
traces of speculation that still remained among the
Stoics showed that the current of men's thought had
taken a new direction. Their conceptions of the
ultimate principles had become materialised. The
universe was regarded as a living being, endowed
with the highest reason[1], and the existence of an
ideal world beyond it was no longer held.

The importance of the Stoics in the history of
philosophy is considerable. When Greek philosophy
was transplanted to Rome, it was Stoicism that found
the new soil most congenial, as the long list of famous
Stoics during the first two centuries of the Empire

[1] Diog. VII. 139; R. P. p. 406.

bears witness. But the Neoplatonic revival in the
third century was, in reality as well as in name, a
reaction to the earlier system of Plato, and owed
little or nothing to Stoic speculation. Indirectly
however the severe Stoic teaching upon morality
paved the way for the lofty mysticism of Plotinus,
and it is of interest to note that the Stoics were the
first school to develope the system of allegorical
interpretation. Mystical interpretations of special
points had already been given by Democritus and by
Metrodorus of Lampsacus[1], as well as by some of
the Cynics; but the method had not before been
systematically applied to the whole field of popular
superstition.

Under the Roman Empire Stoicism continued to
be the dominant philosophical system until the latter
half of the second century of the Christian era. But
before discussing the schools that took its place, we
must turn back for a moment, to trace the rise of a
new stream of speculation, which had begun to
exercise a considerable influence upon the general
current of men's thought. We cannot here enter
fully into the origin either of the Jewish colony at
Alexandria, or of the philosophical school which it
produced. Suffice it to say that the Alexandrian
Jews entered readily into the intellectual life of the
place: they welcomed Greek philosophy as a further
revelation in the light of which the records of the Old
Testament received a new meaning. In particular
the personifications of the Word and Wisdom of God,
which had been described with gradually increasing

[1] Drummond I. p. 121.

clearness by the writers of some of the later books of
the Old Testament, now found a counterpart in the
conceptions of Plato and the other Greek philosophers.
These conceptions the Jewish writers developed in the
light of the strong and pure monotheism of their own
religion, and thus gave rise to the Jewish-Alexandrian
school of philosophy. The most distinguished representative of this school was Philo, whose period of
literary activity seems to have closed about the year
40 A.D. He can hardly be called a great or original
thinker : his system lacks cohesion and is often self-
contradictory : but he is a writer of real importance,
since he marks the first beginnings of a return from
Stoic and Aristotelian teaching towards Platonic
philosophy. It is however correct to say that " Philo
inaugurated Neoplatonism[1]." Nearly two centuries
had yet to elapse before Plotinus took up the study
of philosophy, and it is difficult to find, between
Philo and Ammonius Saccas, a series of philosophers
sufficiently connected to deserve the name of a school.
He was rather a fore-runner, the effects of whose work
were not immediately visible, though destined in after
years to be of the greatest importance.

The teaching of Philo is mainly given in the form
of comments upon various texts out of the Old
Testament. To this peculiarity of form may in part
be ascribed the inconsistencies and general lack of
cohesion to which allusion has already been made.
By adopting it, Philo deprives himself of the opportunity for giving a single exposition of his whole
system, and he is moreover led into the habit of

[1] Crozier, vol. I. p. 70 and p. 450.

expounding each verse to the best of his ability, regardless of what he may have said on the same subject in connexion with another passage.

A few words may be added on the points at which the teaching of Philo approximates most closely to that of the Neoplatonists. Foremost among these stand his conceptions of God, the Logos, and the Powers. Philo is never tired of asserting the existence and the unity of God, in opposition to the views of atheists and polytheists alike. God however is incomprehensible[1]. He is one, He is simple, He is unchangeable, and He is eternal ; but beyond these somewhat negative attributes, man is unable to describe Him, and even the patriarchs were ignorant of His Name. The similarity of this doctrine to Plotinus' conception of The One is obvious. It would seem that Philo derived it, not from Plato nor yet entirely from the Old Testament, but rather from the Old Testament read in the spirit of Plato.

The mediator between God and Man is the Logos[2]. The titles under which He is mentioned indicate the high position which He held in Philo's system. He is called the First-born Son of God[3], the Eldest Angel, the Archangel, the Name or the Image of God, and again, Man in the Image of God. At the same time it is not easy to determine the precise conception that Philo wishes to convey. The Logos is described in one passage as at once the source and the sum of the Powers ; elsewhere as the intelligible

[1] Herriot, *Philon le Juif*, pp. 206 ff.

[2] Herriot, pp. 237 ff.

[3] Philo, *De Conf. Ling.* 28. p. 427 Mang.

world[1], the sum of the Angels or of the Ideas and
again as the divine spirit. At one time He seems
to have a distinct personality, at another, merely to
express the relation in which God stands to the world.
The fact is that Philo deals throughout in metaphors
rather than definitions. He has not formed, in his
own mind, a perfectly distinct conception of the
Logos, and the description which he gives is somewhat
confused in consequence.

The same criticism may be passed upon Philo's
account of the Powers[2]. At one time he seems to
regard them as personified attributes of the Supreme
Being, whether in His aspect of Creator, when we
speak of Him as God, or of Ruler, when we call Him
Lord. At another time he approaches very closely to
the Platonic conception of the Ideas, on the model of
which the world around us was created, whilst in a
third group of passages he identifies the Powers with
the Angels. It may be noticed that Philo seems here
to hover between Platonic and Aristotelian teaching,
and that he anticipates the position adopted by
Plotinus. He follows Plato in assigning an actual
existence to the Ideas, and in speaking of the
intelligible world : but, like Plotinus, he also adopts a
definitely Aristotelian position when he places the
Ideas within the Logos.

With regard to cosmology, Philo accepts the
teaching of Plato[3]. He explicitly rejects both the
Aristotelian view that this world had no beginning

---

[1] Philo, *De Opif. Mundi*, 6. p. 5 Mang.

[2] Herriot, pp. 241 ff.

[3] Herriot, pp. 220 ff. ; cf. *De Incorrupt. Mundi*, 3.

and will have no end, and that of the Stoics, who
believed that the present order of things would one
day be destroyed by fire. He maintains that the
world was created, and thus had a beginning, but that,
once created, it is eternal. He adds moreover[1], like
Plato, and for the reasons which Plato adduces, that
there can be no other physical world than that in
which we live. It is in the highest degree improbable
that God would create a world inferior or even similar
to this one, and it is equally clear that if He had been
able to create a better, He would already have done so.

One other point in Philo's teaching demands a
word in passing[2]. He distinguishes four classes of
"ecstasy." The first is ordinary madness. The second
consists of sudden astonishment such as that with
which Isaac was filled when Esau claimed his blessing.
The third class he describes as the calm state of the
reason which resembles the deep sleep which fell
upon Adam: whilst to the fourth class belongs the
inspiration of the prophets, which Philo himself
professes to have at times experienced. It is to be
remarked that the "ecstasy" of Plotinus is not
identical with the fourth or highest class, but is more
nearly akin to the third in Philo's series. This
example illustrates the characteristic difference that
runs through the whole systems of Plotinus and
Philo, for the latter never permits himself to be so far
carried away by his philosophy as to forget that he is
a Jew, or to enunciate doctrines inconsistent with his
interpretation of the Old Testament scriptures.

[1] Herriot, p. 234.
[2] Herriot, p. 194; *Quis rer. div. heres sit.* 51. 52. p. 509 Mang.

It should be added that Philo is not entirely free
from the Pythagoreanism which contributes so large
a share to the philosophy of the first four centuries
after Christ[1]. To the modern reader, his mystical
speculations on the subject of number appear to be
meaningless and fantastic, but they are thoroughly
characteristic of the age in which they are written.
Numerical mysticism does not play a prominent part
in the philosophy of Plato, although instances of it
are to be found, but out of those who endeavoured in
after years to revive his teaching, there were few who
succeeded in resisting the attraction which speculation
of this kind seems to have exercised.

Another "fore-runner," who still hardly deserves
the title of Neoplatonist, was Plutarch of Chaeronea.
He too was opposed to Stoic doctrines and drew his
inspiration from the writings of Plato. He held that
there are two first principles[2], God and Matter, the
giver and the receiver of form respectively, and
between them, the Ideas, or patterns according to
which the world was made. For Matter, though not
in itself good, is indifferent, and is evil only in so far
as it is permeated by the evil principle which is the
cause of all disorder, and to which Plutarch gives the
title of the World-soul[3]. The system of Plutarch is
less elaborate and less thorough than that of Plotinus,
though in some respects he directly anticipates the
doctrines of the Neoplatonists. He definitely maintains, for example, the existence of both gods and
daemons[4], and in his explanation of the "daemon" of

[1] Herriot, pp. 261 ff.   [2] *De Is. et Osir.* 45. p. 369; R.P. p. 508.
[3] *De An. Procr.* 5. p. 1014.   [4] R.P. p. 510.

Socrates, he clearly takes up the position afterwards adopted by Plotinus, that the true philosopher should base his teaching not upon logical deduction but on direct intuition[1].

It only remains to enumerate the chief philosophers who occur in the century immediately preceding the appearance of Ammonius Saccas. After the time of Marcus Aurelius, the popularity of Stoicism declined, and Neopythagoreanism became the most fashionable form of philosophy. It was characterized by a love of numerical speculation and a somewhat vague mysticism, based on the study of writings, authentic or spurious, attributed to Pythagoras and his school. The most illustrious name in this period is that of Numenius of Apamea, whose famous description of Plato as the Attic Moses[2] illustrates at once his ignorance of the true character of Plato and Moses alike, and his desire to illustrate the affinity that exists between all seekers after truth, to whatever nationality or religion they may belong. It is however more important for our present purpose to notice that Numenius distinguished three gods—the first subsisting in undisturbed self-contemplation, the second and third being the creator and the creation respectively. He also recognised a twofold division of the human soul, into rational and irrational elements. Of these, the former contemplates the deity, whilst the latter renders the soul capable of union with a material body.

The second century also witnessed the rise of a

---

[1] Cf. Maurice, *Moral and Metaphysical Philosophy*, p. 284.
[2] Suidas; R. P. p. 512; Euseb. *Praep. Ev.* 9. 6, 11. 10.

school of sceptics, of whom Sextus Empiricus was
the most considerable; and mention must also be
made of Celsus[1], the great antagonist of Origen. The
Sceptics however need not detain us, and though
Celsus is said to have been a Platonist, the extant
fragments of his work contain but little constructive
philosophy.

It is scarcely necessary to say more about the
general condition of the world of thought at the
beginning of the third century. There was no
teacher of commanding genius, and no school that
could lay claim to any degree of originality or creative
power. We find on all sides an appeal to antiquity,
which meets us in the realms of religion and philosophy alike, and contributes to the popularity both of
Egyptian worship and of Pythagorean teaching. But
the appeal was shallow and uncritical, and the results
were correspondingly barren. Authority took the
place of argument, and progress was held to consist
in tedious elaboration of detail. Orientalism too
exercised a strange fascination over men's minds.
Philostratus described how Apollonius of Tyana had
journeyed to India, to converse with the Brahmins
and other wise men of the East, and it is probable
that there were others, besides Plotinus, who endeavoured to follow his example. Above all, the
spirit of syncretism, whose influence in matters of
religion has already been mentioned, was no less
powerful in the region of philosophy. The aim of
the philosophers was to unite the teachings of all the

---

[1] Cf. Ueberweg, p. 237.

great masters of old; to reconcile Plato with Stoicism, Aristotle with Pythagoreanism and by a judicious combination of these diverse elements, to arrive at a system which should represent, not the teaching of this or that school, but the accumulated wisdom of the human race.

CHAPTER III

THE FIRST BEGINNINGS OF CHRISTIAN PHILOSOPHY

IN the chapter just concluded it will perhaps have been noticed that there is no mention of Christian philosophy. There are the names of Greek philosophers in abundance : something too will be found about the Roman and Jewish schools, but of Christian philosophy as such, nothing has been said. Hence it will be well, before proceeding to discuss the system of Plotinus and the history of his school, to consider briefly what had been the relations between Christianity and philosophy during the first two centuries of our era, and what was the state of things existing at the beginning of the period with which we are concerned.

Now in the first place, there can be no doubt that Christian teaching, as set forth in the New Testament, appealed, and was intended to appeal, not merely to the poor and ignorant but to men of an intellectual and literary bent. St Paul, when preaching at Athens, did not hesitate to address himself to the philosophers, who in their turn, until he excited their derision by speaking of our Lord's Resurrection, were

ready enough to give him a hearing. Nor is this
an isolated case. Alike in the writings of St Paul
and in the Epistle to the Hebrews there are many
passages which show that there must have been in
the Early Church a large number of persons interested
in speculations upon the nature and work of Christ,
and capable of following a theological discussion.
Above all, the words of our Lord Himself, as recorded
in St John's Gospel and elsewhere, express truths
that far transcend all the metaphysical teachings of
the Schools.

But then there comes a drop. The difference, in
point of intellectual level, between the books of the
New Testament and those of the Apostolic Fathers,
is extraordinary. The latter deal almost exclusively
with practical matters: where they attempt to give
an allegorical interpretation, the effect is usually
puerile and grotesque. We search in vain for anything approaching the grandeur of the prologue to
St John's Gospel or the opening chapter of the
Epistle to the Hebrews. It is as though the whole
of the philosophical side of Christianity had been
forgotten.

Now it is probable that a variety of causes
contributed to this result[1]. The age of persecution
had by this time fairly begun. It had become
obvious that persecution was to be the settled policy
of the Roman government towards the Church, and
that fact would of itself tend to make men lay stress
on the practical rather than the philosophical side of
the faith. Again, the death of Philo and the con-

---

[1] Cf. de Faye, *Clément d'Alexandrie*, pp. 119 ff.

sequent decay of the Jewish-Alexandrian system removed one of the greatest incitements to the development of Christian philosophy. Moreover the destruction of Jerusalem served to emphasize what was already becoming obvious, that the main work of the Church must lie, not in the recovery of the Jews but in the conversion of the Gentiles: and in this wide field of action there were preliminary victories to be won in the sphere of common life before Christianity could venture to measure swords with the great schools of heathen thought.

The first attempts to give a philosophical bent to Christian speculation were not encouraging. They are to be found in the swarm of Gnostic heresies with which the Church was compelled to deal in the first two centuries of her history. One and all, the Gnostics claimed to be setting forth a form of the faith truer and more philosophical than that to which ordinary Christians were accustomed, but they went astray through failing to grasp what are the fundamental truths of Christianity, and what the limits outside which speculation ceases to be Christian. So that in one way it is possible that the Gnostics actually retarded the reconciliation between Church and School, for the upholders of the true faith may well have thought it wisest to avoid unnecessary speculation and to refuse the study of philosophy in any shape or form.

But this state of things could not last for ever. Gradually, as time went on, the Church began to attract men of culture, and by the year 150 A.D. we find Justin Martyr suggesting that philosophy should be regarded as God's revelation to the Greeks, and claiming for Socrates, Plato and the rest, a position not unlike that held by Moses and the prophets under the Jewish dispensation. It is true that the change did not come in a moment. Tatian, the pupil of Justin, hates philosophers of all sorts, and Tertullian makes them responsible for the whole of the Gnostic heresies. But the words of Justin show that the tide is already turning, and prepare us for the development of a new system of speculative Christianity.

Alexandria was the place in which this *rapprochement* between Christianity and philosophy found the most congenial soil. It had been from the first one of the most important centres of literary and intellectual life, and its Museum and libraries, its staff of Professors and classes of students, indeed the whole atmosphere of the place encouraged the growth of a liberal spirit of investigation. It is not surprising therefore to find at Alexandria a great Catechetical School, which did not merely provide elementary instruction for those desirous of admission into the Church, but formed, as it were, " a denominational College by the side of a secular University [1]."

Of the early history of the Catechetical School we know but little[2]. It is probable that it began on a small scale, without any official sanction from the rulers of the Church, and developed gradually as opportunity arose. We find the school in existence, soon after the middle of the second century, under the presidency of Pantaenus[3]; but our information

---

[1] Bigg, *Christian Platonists*, p. 42.   [2] de Faye, p. 31.
[3] Eus. *Hist. Eccl.* 5. 10.

with regard to it is scanty until we reach the days of
Pantaenus' disciple and successor, the famous Clement
of Alexandria.

It would appear that Clement was born, either
at Athens or at Alexandria, about the year 150 A.D.
In his youth he travelled widely, and he must also
have been one of the best read men of his time : at all
events there is no other Christian writer of the first
three centuries who shows so intimate a knowledge of
Greek literature. Unlike Origen, he was not the son
of Christian parents, but his conversion seems to have
resembled that described in Justin's *Dialogue with
Trypho* : the desire for a closer contemplation of the
Divine having led him, first to the study of Plato and
Greek philosophy, then to the Old Testament and
the prophets, and lastly to Christ. It was, in fact, an
intellectual rather than a moral conversion, so that
it is not surprising to find that Clement's love for
philosophy is in no way impaired by his profession of
Christianity.

The earliest of his extant works is addressed to
thoughtful pagans[1]. This is the *Protrepticus*, or
" Hortatory word to the Gentiles," in which Clement
begins by endeavouring to release his reader from
popular superstitions. He deals with Greek myth-
ology, with the public worship of the pagan gods, and
with the Mysteries, and then he proceeds to the
speculations of philosophy. These, attractive as they
are, still create a blank which they cannot entirely
fill. They produce a longing for fuller knowledge,
and for more direct communion with God, which can

[1] de Faye, pp. 54 ff.

be satisfied only by the study of Holy Scripture. There can be little doubt that this gives a true picture of Clement's own conversion, and that it indicates clearly the position which he assigns to Greek philosophy.

Following on the *Protrepticus* come the three books of the *Paedagogus* or " Tutor[1]." The *Protrepticus* sets forth the Logos as the Converter of souls : the *Paedagogus* is intended to describe to the new convert the Logos considered as the Educator of souls. Clement makes no attempt to set forth a complete system of education. He indicates a method, and leaves each individual to formulate his own scheme. The first book describes the need of a *Paedagogus*, the love of Christ for man, and His methods of dealing with men. In the second and third books we find descriptions of the vices of heathen life, and of various forms of wrongdoing which the Christian must avoid.

It was Clement's intention to write a third treatise which was to be styled the " Teacher " and was to contain his system of Christian philosophy. This, however, was never written, and in its place we have eight books of Miscellanies, quaintly described as *Stromates* or " Clothes-bags." That the *Stromates* were not intended to take the place of the Teacher is made clear by a number of passages in which Clement speaks of the latter work as still unwritten[2]. They are to be regarded rather as preliminary essays dealing with parts of the subject, and as such they

---

[1] de Faye, pp. 64 ff.

[2] e.g. *Strom.* 7. 59 end.

are by no means devoid of interest. Thus we may
learn from the elaborate apology with which the first
book opens, that the intellectual and speculative
Christians for whom Clement was writing, were, even
at Alexandria, in a minority. Indeed, so great was
the number of those who shared the view that
philosophy and Greek culture were apt to lead men
to heresy and unbelief, and that it was therefore best
to leave these things alone, that Clement actually
goes out of his way to defend even the practice of
literary composition. He treats these upholders of a
narrower Christianity with unfailing courtesy and
consideration, endeavouring always to convert rather
than to confute them ; and it is to the credit of both
parties that there was never any open breach between
them.

The aim of Clement of Alexandria was to absorb
into his teaching all that was good in Greek thought,
whilst rejecting all that was bad and worthless. To
reject the whole of Greek philosophy, as the majority
of the early Fathers had done, was becoming in-
creasingly difficult and unwise : to accept good and
bad indiscriminately involved serious risk of running
into Gnostic and other heresies.

It was necessary to find some standard, and the
test which Clement adopted was partly ethical and
partly theological. Thus he rejected Epicureanism
altogether[1]. A system, based on Atheism, which
taught that pleasure was the guiding principle of life,
won but scant praise from him. Nor did the Stoics
rank high in his estimation ; for did not they teach

[1] *Protr.* 66 end; *Strom.* I. I.

that God is a corporeal being[1]?   Plato and Pythagoras—the Pythagoras not of history but of legend
—are the two philosophers who excite his greatest
admiration ; but he does not confine himself to the
doctrines of any single school.   Philosophy, according to his definition[2] includes all teaching that
conduces to righteousness and sound learning, and he
accepts all teaching to which this definition can be
applied.

From these diverse elements of philosophy and
Christian doctrine, the theology of Clement was
derived.   It remains for us to enquire how far this
theological system was taken over from the philosophers, and to what extent it was the result of purely
Christian influences.   Broadly speaking the system of
Clement may be divided into three main sections—
his conception of God, his conception of the Logos,
and his ethical teaching.   And in the main, the first
of these sections is largely derived from Plato, the
second from Philo, and the third from Aristotle.

The portions of Plato's philosophy which appealed
most strongly to thinkers of the second and third
centuries were his doctrine of the Ideas and his
conception of God as the Idea of " The Good."   This
doctrine Clement accepts and repeatedly emphasizes
in language that is unmistakeable.   God, he says[3] is
independent of time and space and all physical
limitations.   He is not to be described, unless
metaphorically, in anthropomorphic terms[4], for God is
not man-like, nor has he need of senses like ours.

---

[1] *Strom.* 1. 51.   [2] *Strom.* 1. 37.
[3] *Strom.* 2. 6.   [4] *Strom.* 4. 153, 7. 37.

Clement even goes beyond the language of Plato and states[1] that God transcends not merely the physical but even the intelligible world. He is devoid of passions, and can be defined only as pure Being. At the same time it must not be thought that Clement's conception of God is derived exclusively from Platonic sources. When describing the goodness of God, he goes far beyond the philosophers, and adds touches that are unmistakeably Christian, telling us[2] that God does not emit goodness automatically and of necessity, as a fire emits heat, the process is voluntary and conscious. We have here escaped from the conception of God as a mere philosophical abstraction, and passed to the Christian doctrine of a wise and loving Father.

It is unnecessary to enter upon a detailed discussion of the two remaining sections of Clement's system. His doctrine of the Logos is in great measure identical with that of Philo : but here too Clement adds touches which make it plain that he is describing no mere hypothetical being, but the Word Who became flesh for the redemption of the world. And it is the same with his ethical teaching. This is centred in the person of the true Gnostic[3], who is in many respects similar to the "Wise Man" of Stoic tradition. But, even here, Christian Love as well as Knowledge, forms one of the mainsprings of the ideal character.

The foregoing account will make sufficiently clear the attitude of the Christian Church towards the great schools of Greek thought in the years that

---

[1] *Strom.* 5. 39.   [2] *Strom.* 7. 42.   [3] *Strom.* 7. 1 ff.

immediately precede the rise of Neoplatonism. The vast majority of Christians had little taste for philosophy, but a minority, small in numbers though of no mean ability, was endeavouring to claim for Christianity the fruits of Greek speculation. In a previous chapter some attempt has been made to point out what portions of each system were incorporated in the teaching of the Neoplatonists. It is not impossible that the work of Clement was known to the founders of that School—indeed if there is any truth in the story that Ammonius Saccas was at one time a Christian[1], it can hardly have been otherwise. And there are close analogies to be traced in some points of detail between the doctrines of Clement and of Plotinus. It may well be, for instance, that Clement's description of the beatific vision[2] influenced Plotinus in his conception of ecstasy, and that there is some connexion between the Christian Father's description of the Holy Trinity[3] and that later enunciated by the great Neoplatonist. We may notice however that such indebtedness is nowhere acknowledged, indeed if it exists it has been carefully concealed, for in the writings of Plotinus there is not a single reference either to the historical facts on which the Christian faith rests, or to the theological speculations that have been based upon them.

---

[1] Porph. apud Eus. *Hist. Eccl.* 6. 19.
[2] *Strom.* 7. 12, 13.   [3] e.g. *Strom.* 4. 158.

CHAPTER IV

THE HISTORY OF NEOPLATONISM

IN the foregoing pages an attempt has been made to give a general sketch of the prevailing conditions of thought, alike in religion and philosophy, in the period immediately preceding the first appearance of Neoplatonism. In the present chapter it is proposed to give a brief account of the external history of the school, together with the names and dates of the great leaders of Neoplatonic thought, and the chief contemporary Christian writers, pointing out the broad relations between Christianity and philosophy at each stage of the history. In this way we may hope to obtain a general impression of the history of the school, which will serve to place the more detailed discussions of the various stages in their true perspective.

The founder of the school was Ammonius Saccas. Of him and of his teaching we have but little information, and of that little, much is by no means certain. According to Porphyry[1] he was born at Alexandria

---

[1] Eus. *Hist. Eccl.* 6. 19.

of Christian parents: he was himself a Christian in his younger days, but afterwards reverted to paganism. This account is quoted by Eusebius, who proceeds to say that the story of his apostasy is a fabrication. The Christian writers do not claim Ammonius as an ally, but apparently they are anxious to prevent the apologists of paganism from making capital out of the story that the first great Neoplatonist had been converted from Christianity to the purer faith of his pagan fellow-countrymen[1]. His second name is said to be an abbreviated form of Saccophorus and to be derived from the fact that for some time he made his living as a porter. The dates of his birth and death are both unknown, but he must have begun lecturing in or before 231 A.D., since in that year his lectures were attended by Plotinus[2], the most illustrious of his pupils. The other disciples of Ammonius whose names have been preserved, include Longinus, the rhetorician long supposed to be the author of the treatise *De Sublimitate*, the great Christian writer Origenes Adamantius, besides another Origenes, and Herennius, of whom nothing further is known. Like Socrates in earlier days, Ammonius wrote no books; and there is even a story that he forbade his pupils to divulge his teaching. It is therefore difficult to form an opinion upon his merits as a philosopher, since we cannot say how far the doctrines of Plotinus were new, and how far derived from his master.

---

[1] Maurice, *Moral and Metaphysical Philosophy*, p. 316.
[2] Porph. *Vit. Plot.* 3.

i

Plotinus succeeded him as the head of the new school. With regard to this philosopher we have a considerable amount of information, since, in addition to a series of fifty-four treatises from his pen, we possess a memoir of him written by Porphyry, his favourite disciple and literary executor. From this document and from the notices in Eunapius, *Vitae Philosophorum*, we gather the following facts. He was born at Lycopolis in Egypt, about the year 203 A.D.[1] and he commenced the study of philosophy at the age of 28. After attending the lectures of Ammonius for eleven years, he joined Gordianus' expedition to the East in the year 242, hoping thereby to be able to study the philosophy of Persia. The expedition however was a failure. Gordianus was killed, and Plotinus, after barely escaping with his life, made his way first to Antioch, and soon after-wards to Rome. Herennius and Origenes had already broken the compact to reveal none of their master's teaching : and finally Plotinus, feeling him-self no longer bound to observe it, began to frame his discourses on the lectures of Ammonius. Following the example however of his master, he delivered his teaching solely in an oral form until the year 262 A.D.[2], when he was persuaded to write twenty-one treatises for private circulation, and in the next six years he wrote twenty-four more. Nine more were written before his death in 269 A.D., and the whole series of fifty-four treatises was subsequently arranged and

[1] *Vit. Plot.* 2, 3 ; Suidas, *Plotinus*.   [2] *Vit. Plot.* 4—6.

edited by Porphyry, forming the six *Enneads* which we still possess.

His system[1] has for its object the search for the first principles of the universe, and aims at a systematic exposition of the origin and nature of the world: whilst, side by side with this, comes his practical aim, to enable each individual man to rise to the highest development of his nature, and so to proceed ultimately to immediate union with "the divine." His method is eclectic: indeed there is hardly a branch of Greek or Roman speculation, from which he does not levy some contribution. His teaching however is no mere re-statement of current philosophy: it is a return to the original doctrines of Plato. At the same time these are read in the spirit of the age, so that while some elements are neglected, others are sometimes pressed further towards their logical conclusions than in the dialogues of Plato himself.

It is to be noticed that Plotinus does not attempt to establish his fundamental doctrines by argument. The highest knowledge, according to his view, is attained not through logical deduction but by pure intuition: and he therefore enunciates his system without any endeavour to prove it. In so doing he is merely following the fashion of his time. The great popularity of " Mysteries," to which reference has already been made, is an indication of men's readiness to accept mystical teaching about the future state of the soul, upon the bare authority of their instructors ; and although there is no evidence that Plotinus encouraged attendance at such rites, it may well be

[1] Cf. Whittaker, *The Neoplatonists*, c. v.

that the form in which his teaching has come down to us, was affected by the prevalence of such "Mysteries" and by the spirit of obedience to authority which it indicates. It is however to be remembered that Plotinus was a speaker rather than a writer, and it is possible that in his lectures he may have adduced arguments which he did not include in his written works.

The system revolves about the idea of a threefold principle, which appears alike in the universe around us and in our own human nature. The Deity Himself is threefold, the second principle emanating from the first and the third from the second. The first principle[1] is variously styled τὸ ὄν, τὸ ἀγαθόν, τὸ ἕν,— essential Existence, Goodness, Unity : the second is νοῦς, or Universal Mind[2], the creative principle of the world of Ideas, whilst the third is ψυχή the World-soul. This like Mind is immaterial, but standing as it does between Mind and the material world, it has elected to become disintegrated, and united with the world of phenomena. The objects created by this World-soul are themselves souls of various kinds[3], including those of men : and these souls are capable either of rising to union with their source, or of sinking to wallow blindly in their material environment.

Below this Trinity comes φύσις or Nature, still a creative principle, but on a lower level, as being directly connected with matter[4]. Creation is effected, according to Plotinus, by a process of contemplation.

[1] Cf. *Enn.* 2. 9. 1, 5. 2. 1.   [2] *Enn.* 5. 9. 6.
[3] *Enn.* 5. 2. 2.   [4] *Enn.* 4. 4. 13.

The Mind contemplates in The One that which is possible[1], and by continual contemplation, yet ever with fresh difference, it produces all that truly exists, that is to say the Universe of Ideas. Similarly it is by contemplation that the Soul creates, but, inasmuch as it contemplates The One, not directly but through the medium of the Mind, the objects created by it stand on a lower level than those created by the Mind. And in like manner Nature gives form to formless matter, and thus creates the physical world.

Matter is regarded as indestructible, and as existing before the present world[2]. Its existence however is negative rather than positive, for apart from reason it is formless and barren : indeed, the forms which matter assumes in the physical world are in all cases due, not to itself, but to reason. Plotinus argues[3] against those who maintained that Plato's Matter signified empty space, but he agrees with most Platonists in holding that neither the beginning nor the end of the world can be found in time, and that in this sense the universe is eternal. The soul of the universe, like the soul of the individual, is regarded as in some sense bound up with its material surroundings ; so that, to a certain extent, it is in a real sense subject to Necessity or Destiny. Rational action however is always from within, so that virtue is always free[4]. The object of the World-soul is so to pervade this universe as to bring all the parts into harmony. But in practice we find discord, resulting in constant change, and the absence of all except

---

[1] *Enn.* 5. 9. 6.   [2] *Enn.* 2. 4. 5.   [3] *Enn.* 2. 4. 11.
[4] Whittaker, p. 78 ; *Enn.* 3. 1. 10.

mere illusory existence. Men seek for the Good and
cannot attain to it, and therefore they become unjust.
Evil is a lack of the Good; and, in a universe of
separate existences, the presence of good in one place
implies its absence in another[1]. Now if the presence
of evil in the world be admitted, its prevalence is not
difficult to explain. The world is not perfect: it is
a mixed universe, and most of the souls which it
contains are neither very good nor very bad, but
occupy an intermediate position. Nor is it difficult
to explain the apparent success of bad men. This
is partly due to the inertness of their victims, who
deserve to suffer for not attempting to resist their
attacks, and it is in part explained by the fact that
the wicked are thus led on to reap their own punishment, alike in their moral degradation during their
present life, and in its consequences hereafter[2].

But the problem of the cause of the existence of
evil is not affected by these considerations, and the
solution which Plotinus offers is perhaps the weakest
point in his system. He professes to reject all
Gnostic views of the essential inherence of evil in
Matter, and to believe in a single supreme deity, at
once omnipotent and benevolent. But, when pressed
to explain the existence of evil, he is driven to take
refuge in Gnostic dualism and Gnostic hatred of
things material. The reason that he gives is, that
the universe rests on a substratum of matter[3], the
dark principle, incapable of producing anything
beyond itself, and therefore incapable of adequately
expressing the Good. We may notice that Plotinus'

[1] Whittaker, p. 79.   [2] Whittaker, p. 80.   [3] *Enn.* I. 8. 7.

refusal to allow his portrait to be painted[1], and the shame which he professed to feel at being in the body, are illustrations of the same feeling.

In his psychology Plotinus still adheres to a threefold principle. Man possesses Spirit, Soul, and Body, and thus he has three states of consciousness which correspond to the three spheres of being in the universe. Nor is it surprising to find that the virtues fall into three classes[2], corresponding to the three spheres of existence. In the lowest class are the " political virtues," which are necessary for all men, their aim being the avoidance of evil. In the second class, to which the philosopher alone can attain, are the " cathartic virtues," whose aim is the destruction of the passions[3]. The third and highest form of virtue lies in mystical union with The One. This is what Plotinus calls *Ecstasy*, and it is not a faculty, nor yet a habit, but a state of the soul, to which however man can hope to attain but seldom whilst he is in the body[4]. That Plotinus did believe in the possibility of effecting such union even on earth, there is no doubt ; for we have Porphyry's statement[5] that he had himself attained to it once, in his sixty-eighth year, and that Plotinus, during the seven years of Porphyry's friendship with him, enjoyed it four times. This teaching about ecstasy carries us beyond the realm of philosophy into that of pure mysticism. At the same time it is not without its philosophical basis. Plotinus accepted in its entirety the Platonic doctrine of reminiscence, and the state of ecstasy is

---

[1] Porph. *Vit. Plot.* 1.   [2] Whittaker, p. 94.
[3] *Enn.* 1. 2. 4.   [4] *Enn.* 6. 9. 11.   [5] *Vit. Plot.* 23.

neither more nor less than the temporary realisation of the longing which the spirit feels for its return into the world of Ideas.

Such in brief outline is the system of Plotinus. It is clearer and more definite than any that the Neopythagoreans could offer, and the lofty morality to which it leads commands our respect. It derives an added stateliness from the haughty refusal of Plotinus to be drawn into mere recriminations against the upholders of other systems: indeed, it would seem from Porphyry's account that he preferred to leave to his pupils the task of refuting antagonists, as being unworthy of his own attention. At all events it is noticeable that, out of the fifty-four treatises which he wrote, there is but one[1] which is definitely controversial in character, and this is hardly an exception, since it consists for the most part of a dignified recapitulation of his own views, in the expectation that this alone will be sufficient to refute those of his opponents.

In life and character Plotinus seems to have exercised a peculiar attraction over those with whom he came in contact: it is to be noticed that their enemies do not venture to bring any charge against the personal integrity of either Plotinus or Porphyry: whilst both his generosity and his business capacity are illustrated by his readiness, when need arose, to undertake the guardianship of his friends' children, and by his skilful administration of their property. We are told that he almost succeeded in persuading the Emperor Gallienus to rebuild one of the ruined cities of Campania, and to permit him to have it

[1] *Enn.* 2. 9.

governed on Platonic principles[1]. That he was not entirely free from the superstitions of his time is shown by the story[2] of Olympius' attempt to compass his destruction by means of the stars. The attempt failed, but Plotinus admitted that it had nevertheless caused him some discomfort.

During the latter part of his life he suffered from an internal malady, for which he refused to undergo any regular medical treatment. He submitted however to massage at the hands of his attendants, who prevented the malady from increasing; but at length, losing their services in a time of pestilence, he grew worse, and died[3].

ii

The new leader of the Neoplatonic school was a man of Tyrian descent, born in the year 233 A.D. His original name was Melek or Malchus; and this title was occasionally applied to him throughout his life. He was however more commonly known by one or other of two Greek translations of his Tyrian name—Basileus or Porphyrius[4]. Porphyry was acquainted in his younger days with the Christian Origen[5], and, after studying at Athens under Longinus and Apollonius, he came to Rome in 262 A.D., where he met Plotinus, and after a short period of opposition became his most enthusiastic disciple[6]. At the end of six years he found himself suffering from melancholy, and seemed to be in danger of losing his reason: but, adopting the advice of Plotinus, he

---

[1] *Vit. Plot.* 12.   [2] *Vit. Plot.* 10.   [3] *Vit. Plot.* 2.
[4] *Vit. Plot.* 17.   [5] Eus. *Hist. Eccl.* 6. 19.   [6] *Vit. Plot.* 18.

sought relief in foreign travel, and lived for some time in Sicily[1]. Of the details of his later life we know but little : he returned to Rome, where, perhaps as late as 302 A.D. he married Marcella, a Roman lady, and the widow of a friend[2]. Ten months later he went abroad on what he describes as "business connected with the affairs of the Greeks and the will of the gods[3]." It would seem that he died in Rome in or about the year 305 A.D.

Porphyry was a man of great learning, but of no striking originality. As the biographer and literary executor of Plotinus, he made the exposition and defence of his master's teaching the chief work of his life. His own additions to Neoplatonism dealt, for the most part, with the practical bearing of philosophy. Thus he taught that the cause of evil lies not in the body but in the soul[4], and that the end of all philosophy is holiness. In fact, if Neoplatonism reached its highest perfection in metaphysical speculation under Plotinus, it is Porphyry who marks its highest ethical development. His extant writings are not numerous. The *Life of Plotinus* has already been mentioned, and his other principal works are a *Life of Pythagoras*, a vegetarian treatise in four books "*De abstinentia ab esu animalium*," the "*Sententiae*," containing some of his expositions of Plotinus, a short tract "*de antro Nympharum*," an *Introduction to the Categories of Aristotle*, and two *Letters* addressed respectively to Anebon and Marcella.

It was apparently the intention of Porphyry

---

[1] *Vit. Plot.* 5, 6.　　[2] Porph. *Ad Marc.* 1.
[3] *Ad Marc.* 4.　　[4] *Ad Marc.* 29.

to combine direct opposition to Christianity with
the attitude of superiority to pagan systems which
characterized Plotinus.   He wrote an important
treatise against Christianity[1], which seems to have
formed one of the most serious literary attacks ever
made upon the Church; but his attitude of superiority
to the popular religion was not always maintained.
There was by this time a growing tendency, especially
in the Syrian school of Neoplatonists, to lay stress
upon magical or " theurgical " practices ; and there
are passages in which Porphyry displays a certain
sympathy with this tendency.   He quotes Philo
Byblius[2] to prove that the Greek gods were identical
with those of Persia, and he defends the use of images
even to the extent of giving a mystical interpretation
to the materials of which they were made[3].   But these
passages are the exception rather than the rule.   Porphyry remains too thoroughly Greek to agree with
the Syrian school in considering theurgical rites to
be of primary importance : and in the letter to
Anebon he makes his protest against them.   This
document is addressed to an Egyptian priest, and in
it Porphyry takes up the position of a critic.   He
does not question the existence of the gods, but he
wishes to be convinced that men are right in assigning them to special localities, or in supposing that
they are to be propitiated by special forms of
worship.   The other side replied by issuing the
famous treatise *De Mysteriis*, though it is uncertain

---

[1] Eus. *Hist. Eccl.* 6. 19.

[2] Porph. apud Eus. *Praep. Evang.* 1. 10.

[3] Porph. apud Eus. *Praep. Evang.* 3. 7.

whether this work was known to Porphyry or published only after his death. In any case the book is
definitely styled a reply to Porphyry's letter, and it
may almost be considered the official apology of the
Neoplatonists for their defence, not merely of paganism
in general, but of the actual forms of worship then in
vogue.

The writer professes to be an Egyptian priest[1],
but there is no doubt that he is a Greek and moreover a Neoplatonist. He betrays his Greek origin
both by his general style and by definite references
to sundry points of Greek literature with which a
foreigner would hardly be acquainted. His tone of
authority is in keeping, not only with his assumed
character of Egyptian priest, but also with his position
as defender of ritual and mysticism as parts of a
divine revelation. The range of topics with which
he proposes to deal is startling—Theology and
Theurgy, Philosophy, Ethics, and Teleology—but it
shows what a variety of subjects had by this time
been grouped together under the general head of
Neoplatonism.

We cannot here follow the writer in detail, as
point by point he discusses Porphyry's letter and
parries or refutes one after another of his contentions.
His main positions are these. Like Plotinus he holds
that the existence of the gods is not in the ordinary
sense an object of knowledge, capable of being proved
or disproved by logical methods, and of being grasped
by the rational faculty[2]. It is rather a matter of

---

[1] Cf. Maurice, *Moral and Metaphysical Philosophy*, pp. 333 ff.
[2] *De Mysteriis*, 1. 3.

which all men have an innate and indefinable consciousness, so that the most that argument and reason
can do is to distinguish between the various orders of
the gods. They are not to be called corporeal, though
their essence permeates all physical nature[1]. Nor have
they any need of our sacrifices and prayers, though
these have a real value for men, as links of communication with the divine[2]. Now we must offer prayers
and sacrifices to the lower divinities because, although
worship of The One is infinitely higher and nobler,
yet the possibility of attaining to such worship comes
to very few and even to them it comes but late in
life[3]. Moreover, the lower deities are affected by
prayers, and even by threats, provided that these are
uttered not by mere laymen but by duly qualified
priests[4]. Lastly, it must be remembered that the
theurgist is moved by the highest and purest of
aims: his constant endeavour is to raise man step
by step from his natural state of degradation, till at
length he attains to union with the eternal[5].

This then is the argument brought forward in
defence of polytheism and mystical ritual, and it
illustrates at once the strength and the weakness of
Neoplatonism. It shows how Neoplatonism, when no
longer able to produce a teacher capable of following
in the steps of Plotinus, or even of Porphyry, could
still summon to its aid all that conservatism, which
forms so important a factor in the retardation of any
religious movement; and how, by affording a quasi-

---

[1] *De Myst.* 1. 8, 1. 17.   [2] *De Myst.* 1. 12, 5. 10.
[3] *De Myst.* 5. 22.   [4] *De Myst.* 6. 5.
[5] *De Myst.* 10. 5, 6.

philosophical justification to all forms of pagan worship, it could rally round its standard all who were interested in the preservation of the old system. On the other hand the weakness of Neoplatonism is no less apparent ; for the writer of the *De Mysteriis* has to confess that the highest religion is but for the few, and that with all its boasted comprehensiveness Neoplatonism still lacked the simple universality of the Gospel.

iii

With the death of Porphyry the first chapter in the history of Neoplatonism comes to an end. The early Alexandrian Neoplatonists disappear, and their place is taken by the Syrian school to which reference has already been made. The great representative of this school is Iamblichus, who stands first alike in time and reputation. His importance is shown both by the high position which he enjoyed among his contemporaries and by the respect with which he is mentioned by Proclus a century later. He developed the Oriental side of Neoplatonism, his chief additions being connected with numerical speculations and mysticism. Thus he elaborated a logical series of triads and a theory upon the various orders of the gods. He also made considerable additions to the system of Plotinus[1], inventing a new principle styled " The One without participation " (τὸ ἓν ἀμέθεκτον) which he declared to be superior to The Good, and adding further a series of Intellectual, Supramundane,

---

[1] Cf. Erdmann, *Hist. of Philosophy*, tr. Hough, I. p. 248.

and Mundane deities[1], which he made to correspond respectively to Mind, Soul, and Nature, though superior to them in each instance. The improvement which he endeavoured to bring into the system was twofold. In the first place, there was the refinement which sought to discover principles whose relation to the first principles of Plotinus should be the same as that which exists between the world of ideas and the world of phenomena ; and in the second he was clearly anxious to assert the absolute unity of the first principle whilst retaining the triadic arrangement of the whole system. He therefore elevated The One to a position by itself, and completed the trinity of which Mind and Soul were members by the addition of Nature. To the modern mind this fantastic elaboration of metaphysical detail is a mark of declining power, but there is no doubt that it won for Iamblichus the admiration of the philosophers of his day. He is also famous for the attention which he paid to incantations and other theurgical arts. It may however be doubted whether this was not rather characteristic of the age in which he lived than of the man himself. Iamblichus appears to have lived on into the reign of Constantine, and to have died about the year 330 A.D.

A Neoplatonist of a very different stamp from those who have been described was Hierocles[2]. He

---

[1] θεοὶ νοεροί, ὑπερκόσμιοι, ἐγκόσμιοι.

[2] It is customary among modern writers to class Hierocles of Bithynia with the Neoplatonists, nor have I felt justified in breaking through this rule. At the same time neither Eusebius, in his reply to Hierocles' treatise against the Christians, nor Lactantius, appear definitely to speak of him as a Neoplatonist. His book seems to

was a man of action rather than a man of thought;
and his weapons were more frequently those of the
executioner than those of the dialectician.   He was
born in Caria about the year 275, and we learn from
an inscription that he was governor of Palmyra under
Diocletian and Maximian.   It was perhaps at this
period that he became acquainted with Galerius,
whom he is said to have urged to persecute the
Christians.   From Palmyra he was transferred to
Bithynia in the year 304 A.D., and in the following
year he was again removed to Alexandria.   His
claim to be considered a Neoplatonist indicates the
extent to which the school had become the recognised
apologists of paganism.   His one literary work, of
which the name and a few extracts have been preserved, was called "Plain words for the Christians,"
in which, after bringing forward sundry difficulties
and inconsistencies in the Christian scriptures, he
appears to have compared the life and miracles of
Christ with those of Apollonius of Tyana.   The book
itself is no longer extant, but we possess a treatise
written in reply to it by Eusebius, who declares that
the scriptural difficulties had already been sufficiently
answered by Origen in his writings against Celsus.
Hierocles   showed   himself   throughout   a   constant

have consisted of two parts, a series of Biblical questions similar to
those answered by Origen in his writings against Celsus, and an
elaborate attempt to show that Apollonius, the "godlike man" of
paganism, is greater than Jesus, the Christian God.   Strictly speaking
therefore, Hierocles should be reckoned a Neopythagorean, but by the
beginning of the fourth century the two schools had so far amalgamated
that we shall not be far wrong in including his name among the
Neoplatonists.

5—2

enemy of the Christians; and, as governor of
Bithynia, he became notorious for the zeal and
cruelty with which he carried out Diocletian's edicts
for their persecution.

After the death of Iamblichus there is a gap in the
line of great Neoplatonists. We hear indeed of Sopater
of Apamea, who was put to death by Constantine on
a charge of employing magic to delay the arrival of
the imperial corn ships; and the names of Aedesius
of Cappadocia, Maximus of Ephesus, and Eusebius
of Myndus must not be passed over in silence. But
there is no teacher of commanding force who stands
out pre-eminently as the head of the school.

iv

The next name which arrests our attention is that
of the Emperor Julian. More perhaps than almost
any other character in history, he has been the victim
of circumstance. We speak with respect of Celsus
and Porphyry, recognising that, if they were opponents of Christianity, they were nevertheless men
of honesty, who tried by fair and open argument to
justify their preference for the religion of their
ancestors. But of Julian it is difficult to speak without adding the hateful surname of "The Apostate,"
and without regarding him as a traitor, who persecuted the Church and tried to undo the noble work of
Constantine. What that Christianity was which he
forsook, and how far he is to be considered a persecutor of the Church, are questions which we do not
often attempt to answer. The relation however of
Julian to the Church will be more properly considered

in the next chapter: we are at present concerned only with his positive teaching as a representative of the Neoplatonic school.

As a philosopher, Julian cannot indeed be placed on the same level as Plotinus, but he is to be regarded as one who, by example and precept, brought no discredit on the school of which he was a member. A follower of Iamblichus, he exhibits the defects of that section of Neoplatonism—a certain lack of clearness of thought and a fondness for mysticism. But it is an exaggeration to say that "it is in the Emperor Julian and his philosophic friends that Neoplatonism goes down to its nadir[1]." Julian was neither a relentless persecutor of the Church, like Hierocles, nor was he lost, like Iamblichus, in tedious elaboration of unintelligible speculation. In both of these respects Julian stands on a higher level than his immediate predecessors. He cleared away much of the useless detail with which Neoplatonism had latterly been encumbered, and if we remember the absolute power which the Emperor possessed, and the hatred which Julian undoubtedly felt against the Church, we cannot but be surprised at the moderation which he displayed in the matter of persecution.

Turning to the details of Julian's system, we notice that he does not explicitly accept Plotinus' trinity of first principles[2]. His view of The One is in strict accordance with that of Plotinus, but he has little to say about the other members of the trinity, and the relation in which they stand to The One and to each

---

[1] Dict. Christ. Biog. art. "*Julian*."
[2] Rendall, *The Emperor Julian*, pp. 74 ff.

other. On the other hand he is more explicit than
Plotinus had been upon the subordinate orders of
being. Not content with the distinction between the
world of Ideas and the world of phenomena, he sub-
divides the former by contrasting the Intelligible with
the Intellectual (τὸ νοητόν with τὸ νοερόν), thus obtaining three spheres of being in place of the trinity
of first principles which he neglects. He adopts, in
fact, Iamblichus' teaching in its main outlines, but
simplifies it by omitting the constant repetition
whereby Iamblichus had endeavoured to convey a
clearer impression of the transcendental purity of his
ultimate principles.

According to Julian, the highest sphere emanates
directly from The One, and is occupied by the intelligible gods, chief among whom is the Sun,—not
the visible centre of the solar system, but his ideal
counterpart[1]. In addition to his position as head of
the intelligible world, the Sun occupies the same
position in reference to the intellectual and phenomenal spheres which The One holds with regard
to the intelligible. The place of honour which Julian
assigns to the Sun is doubtless due to Oriental in-
influence; and in particular to that of Mithras-
worship. This view is corroborated by the confusion
which Julian permits himself, consciously or uncon-
sciously, to make between the intelligible sun and the
phenomenal. Below the intelligible and intellectual
gods we reach the cosmical sphere, wherein subsist
the lowest order of gods, the various daemons, good
and evil, and the visible world. Matter is regarded

[1] Rendall, p. 77.

by Julian with as much aversion as it is by Plotinus; unless animated by divine essence it cannot even be apprehended by sense, and the union between matter and soul is brought about exclusively for the benefit of the lower principle.

The system of Julian has been described at somewhat greater length than its philosophical importance might seem to warrant, because it represents the final stage reached by Neoplatonism before the end of the struggle with Christianity. A century and three quarters had yet to elapse before Justinian closed the Neoplatonic schools: but after the time of Julian no real effort was made to re-convert the world to paganism. Neoplatonism adopted a more academical dress: its intimate connexion with pagan myths and pagan forms of worship was no longer prominent, and it retired to a position of dignified seclusion, far removed from all questions of religious controversy.

There is another gap in the history of Neoplatonism after the death of Julian. The school was not dead, for it reappears in the early years of the fifth century both at Athens and at Alexandria; and there is moreover positive evidence for its persistence during the interval at Rome, where St Augustine passed through a period of attachment to Neoplatonism before his conversion and baptism in 387 A.D. But it was in a state of suspended animation. For forty years there was not a single Neoplatonic philosopher of the first rank, the chief names of the period being those of Themistius, Eunapius, and Sallustius the friend of Julian. Themistius however is eminent rather as a rhetorician than as a philosopher, and his

speeches, as well as his paraphrases of Aristotle, are
still extant: whilst the fame of Eunapius rests not
upon his philosophical insight but upon the fact that
he is the biographer of the school. Just as the long
line of Stoics had already been ended by Marcus
Aurelius, so it would almost seem as though Neoplatonism took half a century to recover from the
strain of assuming the purple in the person of Julian.

V

This period of stagnation was followed by the
great revival of Neoplatonism which marked the
opening years of the fifth century. This revival had
two centres of activity, in the universities of Alexandria and Athens. It was essentially academical in
character, so that the writings of the last Neoplatonists
consist mainly of commentaries on the works of Plato
and Aristotle. There was a considerable amount of
inter-communication between the two universities,
and we find more than one of the philosophers of
this period connected with both.

Turning first to the Alexandrian school we are
confronted by two striking figures, both of them
strangely attractive and strangely different from the
various philosophers described above. One is Synesius,
the country gentleman, fond of his books yet no less
fond of sport, ready, when need arose, to take up the
arduous duties of a Christian Bishop, and to wear out
his life on behalf of his people and his country. The
other is his teacher, Hypatia, perhaps the noblest of
those women of culture who grace from time to time
the pages of history, who was brutally murdered by

the ignorant mob of Alexandria, the victim of blind
fanaticism and unproved suspicion.

Of the teaching of Hypatia we know but little:
but it may be gathered from the writings of Synesius
that she followed in the steps of Iamblichus. With
regard however to Synesius we are fortunate in
having no lack of materials from which to form our
judgment. His philosophy is rather of the popular
type[1]. There is a certain vagueness in his expressions
which betrays the hand of the *dilettante*, a vagueness
that is especially noticeable in his Hymns. In some
respects however he rises far above the Neoplatonism
of the fourth century. He explicitly rejects the
employment of theurgical arts, and, even before his
conversion to Christianity, he has clearly little belief
in the pagan gods. The claim which he made for
philosophical freedom of thought, before he permitted
himself to be consecrated Bishop of Ptolemais, is a
matter which will more properly be discussed in the
next chapter.

One other member of the Alexandrian school
must be mentioned before we leave this part of the
subject. This is Hierocles, who was a pupil of
Plutarch at Athens, but who afterwards taught at
Alexandria. His position is interesting, standing as
he does midway between Christianity and the old
religion[2]. He softens down the harsher aspects of
paganism, urging men, for example, to universal
charity, and pointing out the efficacy of prayer. It is
interesting too to notice that, in his view, the belief

---

[1] Nicol, *Synesius*, pp. 81 ff.
[2] Cf. Ueberweg, vol. I. p. 257.

in a future state forms the one argument for morality in the present life. Many of his doctrines are identical with those of Origen,—that, for instance, of the pre-natal existence of the soul—and even where he is most distinctively Neoplatonist, his expressions are often very near those of the Alexandrian Fathers. In his extant works Hierocles does not appear to make any direct reference to Christianity, but whether he is to be reckoned as a tacit opponent of the Church, is not clear.

The leader of the Athenian revival was Plutarch the son of Nestorius, whose pupil Syrianus was the teacher of the more famous Proclus. So far as can be judged from the scanty information which we possess about him, Plutarch's philosophy was distinctly Platonic in its tone[1]. He accepted the trinity of Plotinus—The One, Mind, and Soul—and moreover he distinguished the forms immanent in material things from matter itself. Syrianus on the other hand set himself the task of bringing the Aristotelian and Platonic systems into harmony. In his view the works of Aristotle must be studied as a preparation for those of Plato. The same endeavour to reconcile Plato with Aristotle, and indeed to weld the whole of Greek philosophy into one homogeneous system, occupied the energies of Proclus. To enter fully into the details of his teaching would be to trespass beyond the proper limits of this essay, for the direct influence which the Athenian school exercised upon Christianity was but slight. An account however of Neoplatonism which omitted all reference to the last

[1] Cf. Ueberweg, vol. I. pp. 256 ff.

great teacher of the school would be so manifestly incomplete that it will be best to add a few words on the system of Proclus as compared with those of his predecessors.

According to Proclus, all that exists comes into being through a law of "threefold development[1]." Everything has a state of rest (μονή) from which it issues and to which it returns ; for everything is both like and unlike that from which it is derived. By the action of these three, the state of rest, the issuing forth, and the return, the whole system of the universe is gradually developed. With Proclus, as with Plotinus, the ultimate principle is The One, which he defines in language almost identical with that of the first great Neoplatonic writer. From The One however proceed a number of Unities (ἕναδες) which are gods in the highest sense of the term. Below them come the three spheres of ideal existence, for Proclus, not content with the two divisions already distinguished by Julian, speaks of the Intelligible, the Intelligible-Intellectual (τὸ νοητὸν ἅμα καὶ νοερόν), and the Intellectual spheres[2]. From the Intellectual sphere emanates the Psychical, and below that comes the material world. In his teaching upon the lower spheres of existence Proclus follows Plotinus ; but in the higher flights of his philosophy his system becomes more intricate even than that of Iamblichus. Proclus is said to have laid the greatest stress upon the proper performance of mystical ritual, but in his extant works he does not stand forward, like Julian or

---

[1] Ueberweg, vol. I. p. 257 ; Procl. *Inst. Theol.* cc. 31—38.
[2] Ueberweg, vol. I. p. 258 ; Procl. *Plat. Theol.* 3. 14.

the writer of the *De Mysteriis* as the champion of such observances. He saw that the day for their official recognition was past, and he felt that to call public attention to the subject would only bring his school into discredit and persecution.

Proclus died in 485 A.D. and with him the history of Neoplatonism practically closes. He was succeeded by Marinus, whose speculations were chiefly concerned with the theory of Ideas and with mathematics. One or two other names also deserve to be mentioned, such as that of Simplicius of Cilicia, the commentator on Aristotle, and Boethius, who, by his treatise *De consolatione philosophiae*, his translations from Aristotle and Porphyry, and his commentaries on these and other philosophical works, formed for western scholars their chief link with Greek philosophy until the revival of Classical studies at the time of the Renaissance

Neoplatonism continued to be taught until 529 A.D. when Justinian forbade the delivery of philosophical lectures at Athens, and confiscated the property of the Neoplatonic school. The last chapter of the history is well known. Seven Neoplatonists, including Simplicius and Damascius the last head of the school, emigrated to Persia, hoping to find in the East the Utopia which they had sought in vain at Athens[1]. Sadly disappointed they were fain to return, and in 533 A.D. they were permitted to come back to the Roman Empire, retaining full liberty of belief, though still forbidden to give lectures, or otherwise to propagate their doctrines.

[1] Agath. *Hist.* 2. 30; R. P. p. 566.

vi

Whilst reserving for a later chapter all detailed discussion of the relations between Neoplatonism and Christianity, it will be convenient at this point to add a few words about the Christian writers who belong to the same period as the various leaders of the school. The principal Greek fathers contemporary with Plotinus and Porphyry were Origen, Gregory Thaumaturgus and Methodius. The importance for our present purpose, of Origen, the pupil of Ammonius and the instructor of Porphyry, can hardly be over-rated. His immense grasp of varied knowledge, and his comprehensive breadth of view, are illustrated by the description which Gregory Thaumaturgus has left of the course of instruction which he prescribed for his pupils.

Origen and his followers had much in common with the Neoplatonists. Methodius, on the other hand, was entirely opposed, both to Neoplatonism and to the Origenistic school of Christian speculation. He seems to have been a student of Plato, but he imbibed little of his spirit. He wrote a lengthy reply to Porphyry's attack on Christianity, but this, like the work against which it is directed, we no longer possess. He also wrote more than one treatise against the teaching of Origen, notably against his claim that the Resurrection of the body cannot be interpreted in the sense of a physical resurrection. For Origen himself we are told that he entertained a considerable respect, and the fragments of his writings contain allegorical interpretations of scripture exactly similar to those of Origen.

Of Cyprian and Minucius Felix, the contemporary Latin fathers, little need be said. In the dialogue composed by Minucius Felix, Caecilius, the heathen representative, does not adopt a Neoplatonist attitude. On the contrary, his endeavour to refute the doctrine of the immortality of the soul, and to point out the greater durability of the material world, is distinctly opposed to the teaching of the school. Nor need we linger over the name of Cyprian. There are indeed traces of considerable philosophical power in his writings, but he was too much involved in the practical difficulties connected with the administration of his See to pay much attention to the philosophical revival that was taking place in the heathen world. We pass on to the great Christian father who, like Iamblichus and Hierocles, witnessed the persecution under Diocletian and the subsequent triumph of Christianity. Born soon after the year 260 A.D. and living until 339 A.D. Eusebius of Caesarea forms a link between the age of Plotinus and the age of Julian. His position with regard to Neoplatonism is twofold. Against Neoplatonists as the apologists of paganism the Christian Bishop wages unceasing war : but with Neoplatonism as an abstract system of philosophy Eusebius the scholar has much sympathy.

During the period of the great Arian controversy the Church was too much distracted by her own theological difficulties to pay much attention to philosophical problems outside her pale. A literary attack on Christianity made by Julian was answered

in later days by Cyril of Alexandria, and there are
traces in the writings of Athanasius which show that
the indirect influence of Neoplatonism upon Alexandrian thought was still considerable.

In the last three decades of the fourth century
we find the three Cappadocian fathers, Gregory of
Nazianzus, Gregory of Nyssa, and Basil of Caesarea.
As followers of Origen they represent the side of
Christian speculation which is most nearly allied to
Neoplatonism, and their influence tended steadily
towards the absorption by the Church of Neoplatonic
doctrines.   To the same period belongs Epiphanius,
who became Bishop of Constantia in Cyprus in
367 A.D.   Among the Latin fathers of this generation
there are several whose names ought to be mentioned.
There is Hilary of Poictiers who is noticeable as one
of the earliest supporters of Origen in the west, and
Ambrose, Bishop of Milan, to whose teaching the
conversion of Augustine was largely due.   Somewhat
junior to Hilary and Ambrose, but still belonging to
the same period, we find Rufinus the translator of
Origen, and the two great theologians of Western
Christendom, Augustine and Jerome.   All three lived
on into the fifth century, and all of them helped to
disseminate the knowledge of Christian Platonism in
the Western Church.

With the school of Antioch, whose golden age
falls in the early years of the fifth century, we are
not greatly concerned.   Diodore of Tarsus, Theodore
of Mopsuestia, John Chrysostom, and Theodoret hold
a place of their own among the Fathers of the
Christian Church, but the trend of their thought was

practical rather than philosophical, and they were not greatly influenced by Neoplatonic writers. In the same period we find Synesius, Bishop of Ptolemais, to whom reference has already been made. One other writer must be mentioned before we close—the unknown writer who assumed the title of 'Dionysius the Areopagite.' It will be sufficient at this point to say that these writings bear clear marks of the influence of Proclus, and that they appear to have been composed at the end of the fifth century either at Edessa or under the influence of the Edessene school.

We have now traced the main outlines of the history of Neoplatonism. Its course might almost be taken as an illustration of the law of triadic development enunciated by Proclus. We see it first in the hands of Plotinus, far above all controversy, extending indeed a distant recognition to the pagan system then in vogue, but unfettered by the details, whether of ritual or dogma, which that system implied. We see it next, issuing forth and differing more and more widely from its former self, spending a century in barren controversy and useless persecution. And lastly we see the Return. Neoplatonism desists from the struggle, and becomes once more a lofty system of abstract philosophy, like its first self, and yet unlike, in that its energies are directed less to the perfecting of a system than to the criticism and exegesis of the masterpieces of Plato and Aristotle. And thus its work continued, for though the circle directly affected by Neoplatonism in its last stage was small, yet the influence exerted by the Athenian school was perhaps in the end more important than that of Neoplatonism at any other period of its history. Plotinus may have affected the development of Alexandrian theology ; Julian fought nobly for the losing cause of paganism, but it was left to Boethius to store up for future generations the teaching of his more famous predecessors, and to keep the torch of philosophy alight through the dark ages that were to follow.

CHAPTER V

THE RELATIONS BETWEEN NEOPLATONISM
AND CHRISTIANITY

THE broad features of the relations between Neoplatonism and Christianity have been roughly sketched
in the last chapter. There was at first a period of
apparent friendship. Ammonius may or may not
have been a Christian in his youth, but it seems
certain that the Christian Origen attended his lectures,
and moreover that the Neoplatonist Porphyry had at
one time personal dealings with Origen. This early
period of alliance gave place to a second period of
direct antagonism. Porphyry wrote an important
treatise against the Christians, and the next two
generations saw Hierocles the governor of Bithynia
using every means of persecution against the Church,
and Julian endeavouring to re-establish paganism as
the dominant religion of the Empire, whilst the early
years of the fifth century brought the murder of
Hypatia at the hands of the mob at Alexandria.
But before the end of the fourth century there were
already signs of returning friendship between the
philosophers and the theologians. As early as the
year 387 St Augustine had passed through a period

of attachment to Neoplatonism before his final conversion to Christianity, and if in 415 Hypatia was put
to death by the ignorant fanatics, her pupil Synesius
had already been elevated to the office of a Christian
Bishop. The period of antagonism was followed by
the absorption of various Neoplatonic principles by
Christian writers such as 'Dionysius the Areopagite,'
and the vitality of these principles was evinced centuries later by the appearance of a great teacher like
Joannes Scotus (Erigena), who drew his inspiration
from the study of Neoplatonist writings, and whose
doctrines, if audacious, formed a valuable tonic to the
barren theology of his day.

But it is necessary to enter into a more detailed
discussion of the course of these relations between
Neoplatonism and Christianity, and to trace, as far as
is possible, in what their mutual obligations consisted.

The question has often been discussed, as to the
amount of borrowing that took place between the two
systems in the early period, and the answer given has
usually been that little or no direct borrowing could
be traced, although the indirect influence exercised
by each system upon the other was probably considerable. It is necessary to investigate the nature
and the extent of this indirect influence, and the
traces, if such there be, of direct obligations on either
side.

What then are the facts and probabilities of the
case? There is a general agreement among modern
writers that in a certain sense the rise of Neoplatonism
was the result of the spread of Christianity. There is
no doubt whatever that from the time of Porphyry to

the time of Julian one of the chief objects of the
school was the defence and maintenance of the old
paganism.   The question therefore that arises is this :
was this conflict between the philosophers and the
Christian Church a mere accident, or are we to regard
Neoplatonism as being from the outset an attempt to
reform and centralise the old religion, and to find
some coherent system wherewith to oppose the organized advance of the new faith ?   If the latter view
be correct, if we are to view Neoplatonism as a
deliberate attempt to re-establish paganism on its
own merits, the early stage of its history assumes a
new aspect.   Whatever the attitude of Christianity
might be towards Neoplatonism, Neoplatonism was
essentially opposed to Christianity.   But it does not
therefore follow that it was the best policy for the
Neoplatonists to denounce their opponents.   Another
method was open to them, more diplomatic, and from
their own point of view, more dignified.   Denunciation
of the new sect, whether effective or not, at least
implied its recognition : but to pass it over in silence
was more statesmanlike.

In support of the view here suggested, that
Plotinus by his very silence was aiming a blow
against Christianity, it will be worth while to ex-
amine more closely a work to which allusion has
already been made.   The *Life of Apollonius of Tyana*,
written by Philostratus, is an account of an actual
man, the main lines of whose history correspond with
the broad features of this memoir.   But the notes of
Damis of Nineveh were so transformed by Philostratus that the resulting picture is not that of the

historical Apollonius but of the incarnation of the
religious ideal of the Neopythagorean circle by whom
the book was published.   In this biography there is
no direct reference to Christianity, but as we read the
work of Philostratus we are again and again struck
by its resemblance to the Christian Gospels[1].   In the
first place there is a general similarity of outline.
Apollonius is born, mysteriously, at about the same
date as Jesus Christ: after a period of retirement and
preparation, in which he shows a marvellous religious
precocity, we find a period of public ministry followed
by a persecution which corresponds in some sense to
our Lord's Passion; a species of resurrection, and an
ascension.

There are also numerous analogies in detail.
Apollo's messengers sing at the birth of Apollonius,
just as the angels at Bethlehem hymned the birth of
Christ.   Apollonius too has from the first numerous
enemies who are nevertheless unable to harm him:
he is followed by a chosen band of disciples in whose
ranks we find disaffection and even treason.   He sets
his face steadily to go to Rome in spite of the warn-
ings of his friends that the Emperor is seeking to kill
him.   He is set at nought by the servants of Nero,
just as Jesus was mocked by Herod's soldiers.   He is
accused of performing his miracles by magic and
illegal means—a charge precisely similar to that
brought against Christ.   Like our Lord, too, Apollonius is represented as having constantly driven out
daemons by his mere word.   It is even possible to
compare individual miracles on either side.   A parallel

[1] Réville, *La Religion à Rome sous les Sévères*, pp. 227 ff.

to the devils who entered into the herd of swine is to be traced in the story of a demoniac at Athens, whose evil spirit enters into a statue which it overthrows, and at Rome there is a resuscitation of a dead child which is strangely similar to the raising of Jairus' daughter. Apollonius too appears miraculously to certain followers after his departure from earth, and is clearly represented as being then free from the limitations of material existence.

Nor are the analogies confined to the Gospels. Just as Jesus appeared to Saul on the way to Damascus, Apollonius appears miraculously to a declared adversary whom he converts. Like St Peter, or St Paul at Philippi, he breaks his bonds, and like the disciples at Pentecost he has the gift of tongues.

There is of course a danger of pressing these analogies too far: indeed there are probably several cases in which parallels could be adduced from sources that are admittedly free from all connexion with the Gospels[1]. But the collective weight of the whole series is considerable, and it is difficult to believe that the similarity is not due to conscious imitation. Now it has already been noted that throughout the whole of Philostratus' work there is no direct reference to Christianity, and this too can hardly have been accidental. Is it then unreasonable to suppose that in the brilliant circle which gathered round the Empress Julia Domna there were men capable of devising an attempt to cut away the ground beneath the feet of the Christians, by re-writing the Christian

---

[1] Réville, p. 230.

gospel in the support of paganism, without acknow-
ledgment and without any show of controversy?

The advantage of such a device is obvious. A
work that claimed to be historical would gain access
in quarters where a controversial treatise would be
debarred. It might be possible to gain for Apollonius some share of reverence even among the
Christians themselves. And if this were the editors'
aim the absence of all reference to Jesus Christ
becomes not only possible but natural. To mention
Him with reverence would not suit their purpose; to
introduce Him as coming into conflict with Apollonius
and as being by him vanquished, whether in argument
or in wonder working, must inevitably rouse the suspicions of those very persons whose antagonism they
were most anxious not to excite.

They accordingly produced an account of a man
whose existence no one could question, and whose
character they portrayed in colours so attractive as to
gain a measure of approbation even from their opponents. Round his name they grouped a series of
incidents, copied from the Christian Gospels, but with
sufficient alteration to escape the charge of direct
plagiarism. By this means they hoped to secure the
allegiance of many who admired the Christian faith,
but whose conservatism made them anxious to cling
to the old religion, if only it could be shown to hold
its own against the attacks of its opponent. The lack
of all scientific criticism in the modern sense, among
pagans and Christians alike, secured them from de-
tection. The list of authorities quoted by Philostratus
would more than suffice for the acceptance of all the

miracles here recorded : and, without making their
intention too obvious, it was possible for them to place
in the mouth of Apollonius discourses which tended
steadily to the advancement of pagan conservatism
and pagan tolerance as opposed to the revolutionary
and bigoted teaching of Christianity.

In confirmation of the view here expressed it may
be added, that whether or no it was so intended by
the authors, there can be no doubt that later apologists of paganism did make use of the *Life of
Apollonius* in the way that has been described.
Thus in his *Plain words for the Christians* we find
Hierocles of Bithynia giving a catalogue of the
miracles of Apollonius, and then proceeding "Why
then have I mentioned these events? It is in order
that the reader may compare our reasoned and
weighty judgment of each detail with the vapourings
of the Christians. For we speak of him who has
wrought all these things, not as God, but as a man
divinely gifted ; but they, for the sake of a few paltry
miracles, do not hesitate to call their Jesus God[1]."

The revival promoted by Julia Domna was not
altogether successful. But the spirit which prompted
it survived and reappeared nearly half a century later.
The silence of Plotinus upon the subject of Christianity is difficult to explain until we see that it is
deliberate and intentional. In the whole of his published writings—for Porphyry makes it clear that he
collected and edited all that he was able to find—
Christianity is not once mentioned by name, and the
most careful search has produced hardly a single

---

[1] Quoted by Eus. *c. Hieroc.* c. 2 ; Migne, IV. 797.

instance even of indirect reference[1]. It is scarcely
possible to ascribe this silence to ignorance : Plotinus
was hardly in his grave before Porphyry published an
attack upon the Church based upon a careful study of
Christian writings and practices, and it is moreover
difficult to suppose that he was entirely unacquainted
with the works of Origen, who had been like himself
a pupil of Ammonius Saccas. Nor can we set his
silence down to an idea that the Christians were not
worthy of his criticism. If he condescended to write
a treatise against the Gnostics[2], why did he not deign
to spend a passing thought upon the larger and more
important body of orthodox Christians ?

The very fact that direct reference to Christianity
can nowhere be found, although its indirect influence
seems to be distinctly traceable in Plotinus' system,
points towards intentional concealment of his obligations on the part of the writer. Indeed, it may even
be said that Plotinus is specially careful to avoid
using Christian terminology where he approaches most
nearly to Christian doctrines. Thus it is difficult to
believe that Plotinus' doctrine of Mind ($\nu o \hat{v} s$) is not
connected with Philo's speculations on the Word
($\lambda \acute{o} \gamma o s$). In both alike we find the distinctive theory
that the Platonic Ideas, in accordance with which

[1] In his book upon Neoplatonism, p. 83, Mr Whittaker quotes
Enn. i. 8. 5 as "one of the two or three very slight possible allusions
in the Enneads to orthodox Christianity."

[2] Prof. Bigg in his *Bampton Lectures*, p. 30, speaks of those against
whom Plotinus wrote as "purely heathen Gnostics." They are, however, distinctly classed with the Christians by Porphyry (*Vit. Plot.* c. 16)
and it may be assumed that Plotinus himself placed them in the same
category. For the purposes of my argument the point of importance
lies not in what they were, but in what Plotinus supposed them to be.

the visible world was formed, are contained in this
principle. Yet Plotinus studiously avoids using the
term Logos as the title of the second principle of
his trinity. Now it is not easy to see why Plotinus,
whilst using Philo's doctrine should thus avoid Philo's
terminology, unless he had some reason for so doing:
and the simplest explanation is that the word Logos
had in his view been so contaminated by Christian
associations that he preferred to avoid it altogether,
and to go back to the term of the old Greek philosophy. His practice throughout suggests that the
adoption by the school of the position of apologists
for the old religion was not a later development, but
an essential characteristic of Neoplatonism. The
method changed as time went on. Plotinus endeavoured to secure his aim by haughtily ignoring
the Christians: Porphyry condescended to make a
literary attack upon them: Hierocles would not trust
to literary weapons alone, and supplemented the pen
with the sword: but the attitude of the school remained the same throughout.

If this view be correct: if Neoplatonism was from
the first an endeavour to justify on its own merits the
existence and the supremacy of the old system, it is
not surprising that the search for the direct use of
Christian doctrines by the Neoplatonists has been pro-
ductive of such very scanty results. They naturally
preferred not to parade any obligations to their
opponents under which they might labour: they
sought out from earlier systems of philosophy those
elements which were in keeping with the spirit of
their day, and carefully concealed the principles upon

which their selection was based.   Just as Philostratus
and Julia Domna had corrected and improved the
Gospel story, so Plotinus edited and retouched Christian theology in the light of Platonic philosophy.

i

It is then hardly surprising that we can find no
reference to Christianity in the writings of Plotinus.
But if we attack the problem from the other side,
and seek to discover traces of the use of Neoplatonism
by Christian writers, it is possible that better results
may be found.   The third century was a period in
which Christian speculation was unusually free, and
the great Alexandrine Fathers had no hesitation
about turning to Christian use the resources of pagan
philosophy.   We have already remarked the free use
which Clement of Alexandria makes of the writings
of Plato and Philo: let us now compare the positions
of Plotinus and Origen.   In both alike we see an
attempt to reach a plane of philosophical agreement
above all religious controversy, far removed from all
superstition and ritualism, be it Christian or pagan.
Yet their attitudes are perfectly distinct.   Origen,
when pressed, is essentially a Christian.   He accepts
with the fullest reverence the Christian scriptures.   If
he pleads for freedom to indulge in mystical speculation, he is ready to acknowledge the claim of the
ordinary man to be as truly a member of Christ's
Church as himself; moreover, as a theologian, he
does not often permit his philosophy to appear.
Plotinus on the other hand is essentially a philosopher writing to philosophers.   The audience to

whom he speaks is small and select: in the ordinary
man he takes no interest whatever. Religion in the
popular sense is a subject which he avoids: "the
gods must come to me, not I to them," was his reply
when Amelius invited him to accompany him to a
sacrificial feast[1], and it exactly expressed his attitude
to the popular system. He had no great love for
polytheism, but he thought it the most convenient
system for the mass of mankind, and endeavoured to
point out a philosophical basis upon which it might
be supposed to rest.

Turning now to a more detailed comparison of
the doctrines of Plotinus and Origen, we notice in
the first place that a considerable mass of teaching
was common to them both. The main features of
this common teaching, together with the doctrines
added thereto in Christian theology, are admirably
summarized in the *Confessions* of St Augustine[2].
Writing about the Neoplatonist books of which he
was at one time a student, he tells us that he found
in them, not indeed the words, but the substance of
much of the Christology of St Paul and St John,
with, however, serious gaps. The great eternal
verities described in the opening verses of St John's
Gospel he found set forth by the Neoplatonists, but
all that brings the Christian into close personal contact with the Eternal Son of God was omitted.

"For that before all time and above all time Thy
Only-begotten Son abideth unchangeable and coeternal with Thee, and that of His fulness all souls
receive, in order that they may be blessed, and that

[1] Porph. *Vit. Plot.* 10.   [2] Aug. *Conf.* 7. 9.

by participation of Thy eternal wisdom they may be
renewed in order that they may be wise,—this is
there.   But that in due time He died for the ungodly:
that Thou sparedst not Thy only Son, but deliveredst
Him up for all,—this is not there[1]."

It is much the same with the other great articles
of the Christian faith.   The Unity and the Goodness
of God, and even in some sense the three Persons of
the Holy Trinity are doctrines upon which the Neoplatonist, no less than the Christian theologian, lays
much emphasis.   But the love of a heavenly Father
for His children, and the idea that the very highest
of all Beings could be approached by the humblest of
mankind, are thoughts which we find in Christian
writers alone.

In addition to this partial identity of teaching,
there was some similarity in the methods employed
by Origen and the Neoplatonists.   For example,
Origen was at one, if not with Plotinus himself, at
least with the general practice of the school, in
attaching the highest importance to the allegorical
method of interpretation.   The use of allegorical
interpretation was not new.   It had been employed
by many earlier writers, pagan, Jewish, and Christian
alike, and it arose, not from the particular tenets of
any one school, but from the difficulty which inevitably arises, when books written in one period
and at one stage of civilisation come to be accepted
as sacred, and invested with special reverence by later
generations whose civilisation is more advanced.

But although the mystical method of interpreta-

_____
[1] Aug. *Conf.* 7. 9. 3, trans. Bigg.

tion was not peculiar either to Christianity or to Neoplatonism, the extent to which it was employed by both alike calls for at least a passing reference. The difficulty mentioned above was felt severely by the early Christians.   They had adopted the Old Testament in its entirety: they gloried in the link thus obtained with an almost prehistoric antiquity: but they found themselves in consequence confronted with difficulties which their enemies were not slow to turn to account. If the Old Testament was the Word of God, why did the Christians set aside the whole of the sacrificial enactments of the Law? If God, in the Old Testament, be a Being Whose attributes are Justice, Mercy, and Goodness, what explanation can be given of such texts as " I the Lord thy God am a jealous God, visiting the iniquities of the fathers upon the children, unto the third and fourth generation"; or again, "There is no evil in the city which the Lord hath not done[1]?"

In the same manner, educated heathens were brought face to face with problems of a similar kind. If the various local divinities were all different manifestations of the same God, or members of a vast host, who all owned one supreme deity as their Lord and Master, how was it that Homer described the Gods as quarrelling and even fighting one with another?

The time had not yet come either for the Christian to speak of a "progressive revelation," or for the heathen to work out a theory of the evolution of a gradually deepening conception of the deity. Accordingly, both alike took refuge in the allegorical

---

[1] Ex. 20. 5; Amos 3. 6; Orig. *Philoc.* 1. 8.

method of interpretation, and, once introduced, both alike employed it freely, even in cases where there was no difficulty to be solved. If Origen's explanation of the water-pots at Cana[1] appears to us to be far-fetched and unnecessary, Porphyry's account of the Nymph's Grotto affords a parallel instance on the other side.

But the resemblance between Plotinus and Origen is not limited to their general similarity of standpoint or of method. Definite points of contact, which may be grouped in three classes, are to be traced in the positive teaching of both alike. In the first class we may place the doctrines which are not specially characteristic of the teaching of either Origen or Plotinus, the retention of which serves only to increase the general similarity between the two systems. In the second class may be placed those instances in which there is real harmony between them on points of importance, whilst the third class contains cases in which it would appear that the teaching of Origen, without being identical with that of Plotinus, has been distinctly influenced by Neoplatonic theories. We cannot here do more than refer to one or two examples of each class, but the question is one that deserves more attention and more detailed study than it has hitherto received.

An example of the first group may be found in the view, taken by both alike, that the stars are living beings possessed of souls[2]. Strange as it

---

[1] *Philocalia*, 1. 12.

[2] Whittaker, p. 74; Plot. *Enn.* 4. 4. 22; Westcott, *Religious Thought in the West*, p. 229; Origen, *De Princ.* 1. 7. 3, *Comm. in Joh.* t. 2, c. 17.

sounds to modern ears, this doctrine was by no means new, and as his authority for its truth Origen refers, not to Greek philosophy nor even to Philo, but direct to the Old Testament[1]. Instances of this kind are perhaps of small individual importance, but they increase the bulk of teaching common to both systems—a point that must not be lost sight of, if we are to gain an adequate conception of the relations between them.

More important however is the second class, of which two or three examples may be quoted. The pre-natal existence of the soul is a doctrine which Origen[2] may have derived either from Greek or from Jewish sources: it is even possible to quote the New Testament in support of it[3]. But the theory of the transmigration of souls is one of those bolder flights of imagination which are so characteristic of Origen[4] and it is moreover in the fullest harmony with Neo-platonic thought. We may however observe that whereas Plotinus[5], in a section that recalls the famous passage in Plato's *Republic*[6], accepts the possibility of human souls passing into the bodies of lower animals.

Origen explicitly denies that such a thing is conceivable[7]. It may be added that in later years Proclus adopts the same position as the Christian Fathers, and interprets the story of Er the Armenian allegorically.

[1] Jer. 7. 18; Job 25. 5.　　　　[2] *Comm. in Joh.* 1. 2, c. 30.
[3] S. John 9. 2.
[4] Westcott, *R. T. W.* p. 228; Orig. *De Princ.* 1. 6. 2, 3.
[5] Whittaker, p. 96.　　　　[6] *Enn.* 3. 4. 2.
[7] *De Princ.* 1. 8. 4.

Another instance of the same kind is to be found in the view held by Origen that evil is non-being. In his exposition of the third verse of St John's Gospel[1], he endeavours to support his interpretation by adducing a number of passages from both the Old and the New Testament : but it is obvious that the conception of evil as "that which is not" is derived, not from Scripture, but from philosophy. Origen is careful however to stop short of the view that "that which is not" is identical with matter, or of allowing his philosophy to carry him into any form of Gnosticism.

The third group is perhaps the most interesting of all. We have here to deal, not with direct imitation or adoption of Neoplatonic theories, but with their indirect influence upon doctrines essentially Christian, and to point out how far this influence tended to prevent the Christian teaching, and how far it served to bring out more fully its deeper meaning.

There is in Origen's commentary on St John's Gospel a passage so remarkable as to be worth inserting in full[2]. Speaking of the relation between the Son and the Holy Spirit, Origen says "Perhaps we may say even this, that in order to be freed from the bondage of corruption, the creation, and especially the race of men, needed the incarnation of a blessed and divine Power which should reform all that was on the earth : and that this duty fell, as it were, to the Holy Spirit. But being unable to undertake it, He made the Saviour His substitute, as being alone able to endure so great a struggle. And so, while the

---

[1] *Comm. in Joh.* t. 2, c. 13; cf. Plot. *Enn.* 1. 8. 7.
[2] tom. 2, cap. 11.

Father, as Supreme, sends the Son, the Holy Spirit joins in sending Him and in speeding Him on His way : promising in due time to descend upon the Son of God, and to co-operate with Him in the salvation of mankind."

The boldness of this conception is astounding, and it is clear that no orthodox writer could have ventured a century and a half later to declare one Person of the Holy Trinity to be thus inferior to another. For it is to be noticed that although the Holy Spirit joins in sending the Son and in speeding Him on His way, He does so in consequence of His own inability to perform the office which had fallen to Him. We are not however now concerned with the orthodoxy of Origen's view, but with the source from which it is derived, and if we admit that " Origen was deeply influenced by the new philosophy, which seemed to him to unveil fresh depths in the Bible[1]," the answer to this question is not far to seek. In the Neoplatonic trinity the difference between Mind and Soul is accentuated by the fact that the latter has elected to become united with the world of phenomena[2]. Such union could not but incapacitate soul for the work of redemption, since it is clear that the redeemer must be free from the defects and limitations of that which he redeems.

If this explanation be correct, the case is one in which Origen was led by his Neoplatonist tendencies into something very like heresy. But the passage passed unnoticed. The need for defining the relations between the Persons of the Holy Trinity was not yet felt, and more than a century had still to elapse before the doctrine of the· Holy Spirit attracted much attention.

[1] Westcott, *R. T. IV.* p. 208.   [2] *Enn.* 5. 1. 6.

It is only fair to add another instance, in which Origen's view, fiercely opposed during his lifetime and for many years after his death, is nevertheless in complete agreement with modern thought.

To the Christian and to the Neoplatonist alike, the consummation of man's existence is ultimately to be found in assimilation to God. It is true that this is not a doctrine which was borrowed by the Church from the Neoplatonists: on the contrary it is possible that Neoplatonism was in this matter affected by Christian influences. But the form in which it was cast by Origen may be in part due to Neoplatonism[1]. Thus we notice the earnest protest which Origen makes against the extremely literal interpretation current in his day of the doctrine of the Resurrection of the Body[2]. There will be, he says, a resurrection body, for incorporeity is the prerogative of God alone, but we have St Paul's authority for saying that it will differ from our present body alike in form and in composition as widely as the full grown plant differs from the seed. And this conception of a body, differing indeed from that which we now possess but united to it by the continuance of personality, he fortifies by a reference to the Many Mansions in our Father's House[3]. These are, he maintains, a number of resting places in a continual upward progress, each of which throws a flood of light upon the stage through which the soul has passed, and opens up a new vision of greater mysteries beyond. So we are led on to Resurrection, Judgment, Retribution and

---

[1] Orig. *De Princ.* 2. 11. 6.   [2] Fragment, *De Res. Carnis.*
[3] St John 14. 2.

final Blessedness, each of which Origen describes in careful accordance with the words of Scripture. Thus the Resurrection body, instead of being gross and material, will be of fine incorruptible texture, whilst the complete identity of each person will be preserved. Judgment and Retribution are not arbitrary acts of a capricious tyrant but the unimpeded action of divine law and the just severity of a righteous king; and the final Blessedness so far from being a state of indolent repose will be a vision of divine glory, with an ever growing insight into the infinite mysteries of the divine counsels.

It is true that there is no Neoplatonic doctrine that Origen can here be said to have adopted, and in some particulars he is following in the steps of Clement of Alexandria. Yet it is difficult to believe that his insight is wholly unconnected with the teaching of Plotinus, that "the soul aspires to freedom from the trammels of matter, and that rising ever to higher purity it ultimately comes to nothing else except itself; and thus, not being in any thing else, it is in nothing save in itself[1]." In this way, untrammelled by Neoplatonic dogmas, yet filled with the spirit of reverent speculation which prompted them, Origen has succeeded, "by keeping strictly to the Apostolic language, in anticipating results which we have hardly yet secured[2]." In truth it was by no mere accident that Justinian, who closed the Neoplatonic school at Athens, was also the Emperor who procured a formal condemnation of Origen[3].

[1] *Enn.* 6. 9. 11.   [2] Westcott, *R. T. W.* p. 244.

[3] *Ib.* p. 222.

ii

We cannot however linger over this early period of alliance, but must pass on to the period of direct antagonism, inaugurated by Porphyry and closed by Julian. The struggle thus occupied almost a century, and the plan of campaign was not always the same. Each of the great Neoplatonist leaders, Porphyry and Iamblichus, Hierocles and Julian, had his own characteristic method of dealing with the problem, and it is our task to describe what these methods were, and what the resulting attitude of contemporary Christian writers.

The attitude of Porphyry, alike towards Christianity and towards the popular religion, has already been described, together with the treatise in which the supporters of pagan ritual defended their position. It will be well to remember that much of the language there applied to pagan divinities and pagan ceremonies might with slight modifications be employed with reference to the more mystical side of Christianity. Thus Origen, in his *Commentary on St John's Gospel*, had already said that we must rise from practical to theoretical theology[1], and he had moreover in other points anticipated the writer of the *De Mysteriis*. He speaks of the Unity of God and the diversity of His powers, and adduces scriptural proofs for the existence, below God, of gods, thrones, "Sabai" and the like[2]. In the second book of his *Commentary* he elaborates his system yet further[3]. The highest being is Absolute

---

[1] Orig. *Comm. in Joh.* tom. 1, cap. 16   [2] *Ib.* c. 31.
[3] cc. 2, 3.

God (ὁ θεός, or αὐτόθεος); after Whom come successively the Word (θεός, without the article, or ὁ λόγος), the various Images of God, represented by the sun, moon and stars, and lastly the beings who are gods in name but not in reality. Corresponding to these orders of beings we find a variety of religions. In the lowest class are the worshippers of daemons or idols: in the next, those who worship the powers of nature, but are yet free from idol-worship: above them come the ordinary Christians who "know nothing save Jesus Christ and Him crucified," who are, that is, incapable of rising from the adoration of the Incarnate Word to that of the Eternal; whilst the highest class consists of the favoured few to whom the Word of God has come, and who are capable of worshipping God alone, without the mediation even of the Incarnate Son.

These classes of worship are described as though they were definitely crystallized forms of religion. Origen makes it clear however that they are also stages in men's religious education; that men can and do pass from one to another of them, and that, in order to reach the highest form of worship, each individual must pass through one at least of the lower. To this highest class none but the highest spirits can attain during this present life, but Origen clearly believes that in some future state of existence all men will ultimately be brought into complete communion with God. The whole of his teaching upon this subject is closely allied to that of Philo, who maintains that astronomy has played an important part in the religious education of mankind.

It may of course be said that Origen's philosophy
is as essentially a philosophy of the few as that of
Plotinus himself.   That is in a sense true, for the
inner circle to whom his mystical teaching is addressed
can never have been large.   At the same time there
is a difference between Origen and Plotinus, for
whereas the latter addresses himself solely to philosophers, Origen never entirely loses sight of the
needs of the ordinary Christian.   He usually inserts
a simple exposition of each text for the benefit of
the " man in the congregation[1]" before entering upon
the more imaginative speculation which he considers
necessary for the full interpretation of scripture.

The *De Mysteriis* marks the second stage of the
struggle between Church and School.   In this stage
the plan adopted was not that of attacking the new
system, but of strengthening the old.   Between
Porphyry and Hierocles we hear of no Neoplatonist
who wrote against the Christians, the energies of the
school were devoted rather to the defence and elaboration of theurgical practices.

The next writer of importance with whom we
have to deal is Eusebius.   His twofold relation to
Neoplatonism has been mentioned above, so that we
need not here do more than refer to passages in his
works which bear out what has already been said.
The references to Porphyry in the *Ecclesiastical
History*[2] give us Eusebius' estimate of him as the
opponent of Christianity, who employs abuse instead
of argument, and falsifies the story of Ammonius

[1] ὁ ἐκκλησιαστικός, cf. tom. 6, c. 11 ; tom. 13, c. 44.
[2] Eus. *Hist. Eccl.* 6. 19.

Saccas in order to prove the superior attractions of paganism. In the earlier books of the *Praeparatio Evangelica*[1] we find Eusebius criticizing Porphyry as the apologist of paganism ; pouring contempt on his justification of the use of images, or on his endeavour to account for the existence of the world by means of deities who are themselves dependent upon this world for their very existence.

On the other hand, when dealing with Neoplatonism apart from questions of religious controversy, Eusebius shows a distinct sympathy for the teaching of the school. Of this sympathy one or two examples will here suffice, although it would not be difficult to increase the number. The opening chapter of the *Praeparatio Evangelica* has about it an undoubted ring of Neoplatonism. Eusebius describes the blessings promised by the Gospel as including "all that is dear to the souls that are possessed of intellectual being," whilst his definition of the true piety, and his reference to the Word sent like a ray of dazzling light from God recall to our minds the phraseology of Plotinus[2]. In the later books the indications of sympathy are yet more marked. He speaks for instance of the Platonists as foreshadowing the doctrine of the Holy Trinity[3], and quotes Plotinus upon the immortality of the soul[4].

Before passing on to the Emperor Julian, a word must be said about the attitude of Athanasius towards Neoplatonism. Into the larger question of the Arian

---

[1] Eus. *Praep. Evang.* 3. 7, 3. 9, 3. 4.
[2] *Ib.* 1. 1.   [3] *Ib.* 11. 20, p. 541 d.
[4] *Ib.* 15. 10, p. 811 b.

controversy we cannot enter : we can only note in
passing that the point at issue was no mere theological
quibble : it was the question, whether in spite of the
victory of Christianity over paganism, a new polytheism was yet to be allowed to crush the life out
of Christian teaching, or whether the Church was
strong enough to bear the strain of finding her ranks
suddenly swelled by throngs of new converts each of
whom brought with him a certain residuum of pagan
ideas[1]. The influence of Neoplatonism upon the
course of the controversy seems to have been less
than we might have expected : it does not appear
that the Arians as a party made use of Neoplatonic
doctrines, or that, even at the height of the controversy
the orthodox party broke away from all contact with
the school.

In his *Oration against the Gentiles* Athanasius
speaks in terms which remind us of Origen or
Eusebius, so completely does he reproduce in Christian
form the teaching of Plotinus. The following may
serve for an example[2], "for when the reason of man
doth not converse with bodies, then hath it not any
mixture of the desire which comes from these, but is
wholly at one with itself, as it was at the beginning.
Then, passing through sensible and human things it
becomes raised up, and beholding the Word, sees in
Him also the Father of the Word, delights itself with
the contemplation of Him, and continually renews itself
afresh with the longing after Him : even as the Holy
Scriptures say that man (who in the Hebrew tongue

---

[1] Cf. Maurice, *Moral and Metaphysical Philosophy*, p. 352.
[2] I quote from Maurice, p. 349.

was called Adam) with unashamed boldness maintained his mind towards God, and had intercourse
with the saints in that contemplation of intelligible
things, which he held in the place figuratively termed
by Moses Paradise."

This extract will be sufficient to show that the
greatest of the Nicene Fathers was thoroughly in
sympathy with the higher side of Neoplatonism, a
fact which goes far to explain the absence of appeal
to Neoplatonic doctrine on the part of his opponents.
To confront the teaching of the New Testament with
that of Plotinus would be to abandon all claim to be
considered Christians, and without doing this it was
difficult to show themselves more in sympathy with
Neoplatonism than the orthodox party.

iii

We now reach the last great effort that was made
by the Neoplatonists to oust Christianity from the
position which it had won, and to restore the old
pagan system in its stead.   With regard to the
philosophy of Julian something has been said in an
earlier chapter ; it remains to discuss briefly his
attitude towards the Church.   His aversion to
Christianity is not difficult to explain[1].   The faith
reached him through the agency of insincere teachers :
it was tainted with Arianism, and poisoned by asso-
ciation with the name of Constantius.   On the other
hand paganism could now appeal to his sympathy
as a persecuted religion : it brought with it all the

---

[1] Cf. Rendall, *The Emperor Julian*, pp. 41, 44.

attractions of Greek poetry and Greek philosophy, and was in fact associated with all that was bright in the recollections of his boyhood. From professed adherence to Christianity he passed through Neo-platonism to an attachment to paganism, at first concealed, but after his cousin's death openly avowed.

What then was the policy which Julian adopted towards Christianity? Persecution, so far as was possible, he avoided, but all methods of checking Christianity short of persecution he welcomed. He wrote against the Christians, he forbade Christians to teach the classics, and more striking than either of these methods, he endeavoured to re-model paganism on Christian lines. In his seven books against the Christians[1] he seems to have argued against Christian refusal to recognise the inherence of evil in matter, to have quoted a number of passages from the Old Testament to prove the immorality and impotence of God, and to have subjected the New Testament to the same unsparing criticism. He utterly failed to understand Christianity, and he allowed his prejudice against it to influence the whole of his writings on the subject.

The educational edict was no less a part of the attempt to restore paganism. If the old religion was to recover its ground, it was needful to help it to make a start, and the manifest unfairness, in Julian's eyes, of allowing the classics to be taught by those who refused to accept the gods in whose honour they were written, seemed to justify this ingenious measure of repression. It was doubtless intended to aid the side

[1] Cf. Rendall, pp. 232–6.

of paganism by giving a pagan bias to the whole of the higher education of the Empire as well as by conferring a valuable monopoly upon pagan teachers.

But the most interesting of all Julian's actions were his endeavours to reform paganism. He recognised the enormous superiority of the Christians, in their general standard of morality and in the organization of their Church. In both points Julian attempted to learn a lesson from his opponents. "He introduced an elaborate sacerdotal system. The practices of sacred reading, preaching, praying, antiphonal singing, penance and a strict ecclesiastical discipline were all innovations in pagan ritual. Added to these was a system of organized almsgiving like that to which Julian attributed so much of the success of Christianity ; with the proceeds temples might be restored, the poor succoured, the sick and destitute relieved. Nay, if Gregory's words are more than rhetoric, even monasteries and nunneries, refuges and hospitals, were reared in the name of paganism[1]."

The attempt however failed. Julian had over-estimated the power of heathenism as much as he had underestimated that of Christianity. He hoped that by extending to paganism that patronage which had for the last forty years been given to Christianity, the old religion would be able to assert itself and eject the usurper. But it was too late, and Julian's effort proved to be, not as he had hoped, the dawn of a new day, but the last flicker of paganism before its lamp went out for ever.

[1] Rendall. p. 252.

iv

We have now endeavoured to trace the attitude
of Neoplatonism towards Christianity from the time
of Plotinus to that of Julian. Sometimes the Church
was treated by the School with disdainful silence:
sometimes there was an outbreak of open antagonism;
but the official attitude, if we may use the term, was
never friendly. At the same time there are several
instances of individual pagans who were first attracted
by the teaching of the Neoplatonists, and who
passed from that to a belief in Jesus Christ, finding in
the Gospel something which satisfied them in a way
which the abstract teaching of philosophy was unable
to do. Such a man was Hilary of Poictiers[1]. Born
in Western Gaul at the very beginning of the fourth
century, he was well educated like many other
provincials of his day. He learned Greek, and in
his earlier manhood he studied Neoplatonism; and
thus in middle life he approached Christianity. We
cannot say whether it was before or after his conversion
that he became acquainted with the works of Origen,
but at some period he appears to have been a careful
student, not of Origen only but of Clement and
even of Philo. The way in which he was led on
from Neoplatonism to Christianity may best be
described in his own words[2]: "While my mind was
dwelling on these and on many like thoughts, I
chanced upon the books which, according to the

[1] See E. W. Watson's Introduction, in *Nicene and Post-Nicene Fathers*.

[2] *De Trinitate*, 1. 5, E. W. Watson's trans.

tradition of the Hebrew faith were written by Moses and the prophets; and found in them words spoken by God the Creator, testifying of Himself I AM THAT I AM, and again HE THAT IS hath sent me unto you. I confess that I was amazed to find in them an indication concerning God so exact that it expressed in the terms best adapted to human understanding an unattainable insight into the mystery of the divine nature. For no property of God which the mind can grasp is more characteristic of Him than existence,...and it was worthy of Him to reveal this one thing, that HE IS, as an assurance of His absolute eternity."

Nor does Hilary stand alone, as an educated pagan who passed through Neoplatonism to Christianity. Born half a century later, in 354 A.D., at Thagaste in North Africa, Augustine travelled on almost the same road. He differed indeed from Hilary in that his mother was a Christian, so that he " sucked in the name of Christ with his mother's milk[1]," but Monnica, though a saint, was not an intellectual woman, and for many years she had little influence over her brilliant but wayward son. He followed his own bent. Questions of one kind and another soon began to trouble him, and first of all he turned to the Manicheans for an answer. They offered to solve one half of his difficulties by sweeping away the Old Testament with all its problems, and the other half by declaring that the world is as bad as it can be, so that no man is responsible for his own

[1] Aug. *Conf.* 3. 4.

sins.   But Augustine could not rest satisfied with
this creed for long.   His own common sense, and the
evil lives of some of the Manicheans, decided him to
seek for something better: and in his twenty-ninth
year, when lecturer in Rhetoric at Milan, he began
to apply himself closely to the study of Neoplatonism.
This cleared away his intellectual difficulties, but
still it failed to satisfy him.   The Neoplatonic conception of sin as a pure negation which does not
really affect the inner life and soul of the sinner, and
which can be driven out of the system by a course
of discipline, he felt to be incomplete: and the
sermons of Ambrose, Bishop of Milan, drew him on
to a fuller understanding of the depth and comfort
of the Christian faith.   So he passed on to his baptism
at the age of thirty-two, and four years later he was
ordained.   In 395 he was consecrated Bishop as
coadjutor to Valerius, after whose death in the
following year he became Bishop of the diocese of
Hippo.   This office he continued to hold, up to the
time of his death in 430 A.D.

It will be well to consider the case of Augustine a
little more closely, for we are fortunate in possessing
ample evidence as to the effect produced by Neoplatonism upon his life and thought.   We have in
the first place the detailed account of his conversion
written by himself in the *Confessions* and we also
find in his later writings a mass of material out of
which to form an estimate of the permanence of the
mark left by Neoplatonism upon his theology.

Neoplatonism, as we have seen, was the half-way
house at which Augustine made a stay between

Manicheism and Christianity[1]. At the time of his baptism, and indeed for some years after, its influence upon him was very strong, but gradually his feeling of obligation to the school faded away, and in his later writings we sometimes find him using stern language about the dangers of philosophy[2]. There was however one lesson of enduring value which Augustine owed to the Neoplatonists. It was to them that he owed his first grasp of the doctrine of the Being of God[3]. From the Neoplatonists he would learn about the transcendent greatness of God, how God is so entirely beyond our knowledge that it is better to confess ignorance than rashly to claim that we comprehend Him. It is impossible to describe Him in positive terms, and all that we can do is to define in some directions what He is not[4]. Thus God is simple and unchangeable, incorruptible and eternal, untrammelled by limitations of time and space, ever present, yet always in a spiritual, not in a corporeal sense, infinitely great, infinitely good, infinite in His power and justice[5]. And it is to be noted that not only is Augustine's teaching about the Being of God similar to that of Plotinus, but that there is a close parallelism between the arguments and illustrations whereby the two writers seek to establish their respective positions[6]. It is not too

---

[1] Grandgeorge, *Saint Augustin et le Néo-Platonisme*, p. 149.

[2] e.g. *Serm.* 348; Grandgeorge, p. 28.

[3] *Ib.* p. 60.

[4] Aug. *De Civ. Dei*, 9. 16; *Serm.* 117. 5; *De Trin.* 82.

[5] Cf. Plot. *Enn.* 6. 5. 9, 3. 9. 3, 4. 4. 11, 3. 7. 1; Aug. *Conf.* 1. 2, 11. 31, 12. 11; *De Mus.* 6. 11

[6] Cf. Grandgeorge, p. 70.

much to say that in this department of theology, Augustine's expression of his doctrine was largely coloured by the writings of Plotinus which he had studied.

But Christian doctrine and Augustinian theology carry us beyond bald statements about the attributes of the Deity, and it will be well for us to compare the teaching of Augustine with that of Plotinus on the subject of the Trinity[1]. There is of course at first sight an obvious similarity between Neoplatonism and Christianity in this matter. Both alike speak of the Supreme Being as in some sense threefold. Both alike insist on Existence and Unity and Goodness as the absolute prerogatives of the ultimate source of all being. There is moreover a close resemblance between the terms Mind and Word, Soul and Spirit, which they apply respectively to the second and third manifestations of the One Deity. At the same time, a very little examination will make it plain that this resemblance is only superficial. The very word Subsistence, ὑπόστασις, which is applied by both to the Persons or Principles of the Trinity, is used in different senses. In the writings of Plotinus, it signifies substantial existence, and when the Neoplatonists distinguish between three Subsistences in their trinity, they are emphasizing the very doctrine which the orthodox party in the Arian controversy strained every nerve to refute,— the doctrine that there is a difference of substance between the Father, the Son and the Holy Ghost. On the other hand, when a post-Nicene Father

[1] Cf. Grandgeorge, c. III.

employs the term, he signifies by it a Person, and this in turn is what Plotinus refused to predicate of his first Principles.

And when we go further, and compare the two doctrines in detail, we cannot fail to be struck by the utter absence of love in the Neoplatonic system. Not only is The One absolutely impersonal, but it takes cognizance of nothing except itself. It is true that Mind emanates from The One, and in due course Soul emanates from Mind, but in each case, the superior principle entirely ignores the existence of that below, and looks simply and solely to itself and to that above. There is thus no thought of the mutual Love which subsists between the Three Persons of the Holy Trinity, and the three principles of Neoplatonism are subordinated one to another, and are in no sense coeternal together and coequal[1]. The only real identity of teaching lies in this, that Christian and Neoplatonist alike emphasize the Unity of God, and both alike hold that this unity somehow admits of plurality, and that there is some kind of Trinity connected with the Supreme Being.

It may be remarked that the Christian doctrine of the Holy Trinity is anterior to the rise of Neo-platonism, so that it is not to be imagined that the Church derived her teaching from the philosophers. At the same time it is possible that the writings of Philo and the Neoplatonists helped the Christian Fathers to clear their ideas, when it became necessary to expand and define the doctrine of the Church. There is of course a difference between the stand-

---

[1] Plot. *Enn.* 5. 2. 2.

points of the two, for the Christian dogma is not a philosophical thesis but a verity of revealed religion. But in maintaining the philosophical reasonableness of the doctrine, the Christian apologist found an ally in Plotinus, for part at all events of the struggle; and of his help Augustine is willing to avail himself so far as it goes.

We next pass on to the relations between God and the created world[1]. In the view of Plotinus and of Augustine alike, the world is the result of God's action: but there their agreement ceases. We have seen that the Neoplatonic principles are devoid of love; they are no less devoid of will. It is true that the intelligible world owes its origin to Mind and the physical world has been derived from Soul, but neither of these creative acts is an expression of the will. Each world is rather the inevitable result of the goodness of the creator, the necessary shadow or reflection of the infinite[2]. Plotinus compares the creating principle to a spring or to the life in a tree, and creation to the ripples on the surface of the water, or to the twigs and branches in which the life gives evidence of its presence[3]. To Augustine on the other hand there is no question of necessity or inevitability. The world is in a real sense created, not generated; it owes its existence to the Will of God, and it was made out of nothing[4]. There is in fact no need for the interposition of a series of links between God and matter. We find then in Plotinus

---

[1] Cf. Grandgeorge, c. IV.
[2] Plot. *Enn.* 3. 2. 2.   [3] *Ib.* 3. 8. 10.
[4] Aug. *De Fid. et Symb.* 1. 2; Grandgeorge, p. 110.

three subsistences, emanating one from another, and giving birth to the world by the sheer necessity of their nature, and in Augustine, the creation of the world by the voluntary act of the One God, freely done out of His loving kindness towards His creatures.

It remains to compare the teaching of Plotinus with that of Augustine upon the problem of evil[1]. According to Plotinus, the source of evil in the world is to be found in the inherent qualities of matter. Matter contains elements of change and decay, and it is therefore the absolute antithesis of true existence or goodness.   And just as the world contains elements of good, because it has come into existence through the inevitable working of the goodness of Soul, so, taking as it does its visible form from matter, it contains no less inevitably elements of evil[2].   At the same time, evil is devoid of real existence—it is in fact but a lesser degree of good—so that the physical world, albeit imperfect, is still a true copy of the intelligible.   Indeed the world as a whole is good and happy, and it is as foolish to condemn the whole because parts are faulty, as it would be to condemn the whole human race because it produced a Thersites[3]. Now man's sinfulness is the necessary result of his bodily nature, but this union of soul and body is not entirely evil.   In spite of the tendency to sin, human liberty is safeguarded, for the soul is capable, if it chooses, of detaching itself from the sensible world and turning back towards the intelligible, nor can the body prevent it from so doing.   It is therefore possible for man, by a long course of self-discipline,

[1] Cf. Grandgeorge, c. v.   [2] *Enn.* 3. 2. 2.   [3] *Ib.* 3. 2. 3.

to purify himself, and to rise at last into union with The One[1].

These views of Plotinus made a profound impression on the mind of Augustine. Not only had he himself passed through Manicheism in his earlier years, but after his conversion he was still engaged in combating Gnostic dualism. And in discussing the problem of evil, no less than in maintaining the doctrine of the Holy Trinity, he was always ready to make use of such help as Neoplatonism could supply. Nor was it difficult for him to do so. Church and School alike based their teaching on the doctrine that the world owes its existence to the goodness of God, and in this particular connexion there was no need to draw attention to the difference between Generation and Creation. Accordingly Augustine makes free use of statements and illustrations which recall the teaching of Plotinus. He reminds us that there is abundant evidence of God's good providence in the world, and asserts that the world is indubitably the work of a perfect craftsman[2]. Yet the fact remains that we see evil all around us. How can this be explained? We see it because the world, though good, is not perfect. If it were perfect, it would be incorruptible: were it not good it would be below the possibility of further corruption. And evil, in spite of appearances to the contrary, is devoid of true existence: for, if it possessed true being, it would of necessity be good[3].

Again, like Plotinus, Augustine is confident of the ultimate triumph of good, and like him too he suggests that evil may even be regarded as a factor

[1] *Enn.* 6. 9. 11.   [2] Aug. *De Civ. Dei*, 11. 22.   [3] Aug. *Conf.* 7. 12.

in the progress of mankind. Poverty and sickness
are sometimes conducive to the well-being of the
body, and it may be that our sins actually conduce to
the progress of the universe[1]. At this point however
the Christian Father is faced with a problem from
which the heathen philosopher is free. If this view
be correct, if evil actually leads us on towards good,
why does God punish the guilty? Augustine parries
the question by answering that it is the sin that is
punished, whilst it is the soul that makes the progress.
Indeed it is this system of reward for good and punishment for sin that enables the universe to be as perfect
as it is. For sin is not truly natural to us, but a
voluntary affection of our nature, and in the same
way punishment must be regarded, not indeed as
natural, but as a penal affection consequent upon sin[2].

The key to the whole problem of evil is found by
Augustine and Plotinus alike, in the unbroken chain
of causation which we see in the universe. Nothing
comes to pass by mere chance: everything is the result
of some cause, and everything too produces its own
effect. We must not then complain blindly against the
existence of sin, for sin is the result of free will, and
without free will man would be less perfect than he
is[3]. Indeed the world would fall short of its present
perfection, were it not composed of many different
elements, some of them higher in the scale of being
and some lower. We must not complain because the
earthly sphere is not on the same level as the heavenly,

[1] Aug. *De Ordine*, 2. 4; Plot. *Enn.* 3. 2. 11.
[2] Aug. *De Lib. Arb.* 3. 9. 25.
[3] Plot. *Enn.* 3. 2. 7; Aug. *De Lib. Arb.* 3. 1. 2.

but we might reasonably complain if there were no
heaven for us to gaze at from earth[1]. Evil then has
a legitimate place in the world, but it is simply a
negation, a falling short of the highest possibilities.

There is of course another great section of
Augustine's work to which no reference has as yet
been made—his controversy with the Pelagians upon
the question of Original Sin. But a full discussion of
this subject would carry us far beyond the scope of
the present essay, and it will be sufficient to note that
Augustine's view of original sin does not appear to
be connected with Plotinus' account of the contamina-
tion of the soul due to its descent into matter. But
enough has been said to indicate the extent to which
Augustine was indebted to the Neoplatonists and
the points at which he found their system defective.
It was to him a temporary shelter, where he could
release himself from the entanglements of Manicheism
and make ready for his final conversion to Christianity.
But, that conversion once effected, the influence of
Neoplatonism declined. There was indeed no sudden
break, and to the end of his life Augustine did not
disdain, when necessary, to borrow a weapon from
the Neoplatonic armoury. But the system ceased to
excite his enthusiasm : it had done its work, and
after that it failed to satisfy Augustine as it failed to
conquer the world.

[1] Aug. *De Lib. Arb.* 3. 5. 13.

V

In the earlier part of the present chapter, an attempt has been made to trace the influence which was brought to bear upon the leaders of Christianity by the great representatives of Neoplatonism. It will be well for us, before going further, to consider the influence, less direct but not less important, which Neoplatonism exercised upon the development of Christian thought through the writings of its greatest Christian exponent. The name of Origen has always possessed a remarkable fascination for churchmen of every school, and this fascination is due to a variety of causes. It is in part due to the unique position occupied by Origen in ecclesiastical speculation. There cannot fail to be something interesting about a writer who is denounced as the father of Arianism, and who yet finds a champion in Athanasius. But it is due no less to the simple holiness of his ascetic life, the memory of which survived for centuries, even among those who looked on him as a dangerous heresiarch. "There is a perplexed controversy" writes a German chronicler of the fifteenth century, "in which sundry people engage about Samson, Solomon, Trajan and Origen, whether they were saved or not. That I leave to the Lord[1]."

The position and the teaching were not long suffered to pass unchallenged[2]. Even before his

---

[1] Westcott, *Religious Thought in the West*, p. 224.

[2] See A. W. W. Dale, art. "*Origenistic Controversies*" in Dict. Christ. Biog.

death in 253, attacks were made upon him by
Demetrius, Bishop of Alexandria, who seems twice
to have procured his condemnation. On the first of
these occasions there was no direct reference to
doctrine, the charges preferred dealing simply with
the irregularity of Origen's ordination to the Priesthood. It is however possible that questions of
doctrine formed part of the second attack, when a
gathering of Egyptian Bishops declared that his
ordination was to be considered null and void. But
this sentence, although it is said by Jerome to have
been ratified by the Bishop of Rome, carried but
little real weight. It merely reflected the personal
feelings of Demetrius, and after his death it was soon
forgotten. Heraclas, the successor alike of Origen at
the Catechetical School and of Demetrius as Bishop
of Alexandria, did nothing to express his approval or
disapproval of the condemnation, but Dionysius, who
followed Heraclas in both offices, openly defended
Origen's teaching and character, and in particular
maintained stoutly the value of allegorical interpretation. Among those who came after him at Alexandria
may be mentioned the names of Theognostus, who
wrote several books in imitation of the *De Principiis*,
and Pierius, whose support of Origen's views, alike on
the subordination of the Holy Spirit to the Father
and the Son, and on the pre-natal existence of the
human soul, earned for him the name of "the Second
Origen."

But whilst at Alexandria the influence of Origen
soon reasserted itself, there were other quarters in
which attacks were made upon his teaching. The

treatise published by Methodius of Patara has already
been mentioned.   This was immediately answered by
Pamphilus and Eusebius, who set to work in 306 to
compile a defence of the impugned doctrines.   It is
not necessary to enter into the details of their
argument: suffice it to say that, whilst maintaining
the general orthodoxy of Origen in matters of faith,
they admitted that in cases where the church was
silent, he had indulged in speculations of varying
merits.   Such tentative theories, however, must not
be placed on a level with statements of doctrine, nor
was it fair to stigmatize their author as heretical.

It has been remarked in an earlier chapter that
the direct influence of Neoplatonism upon the Arian
controversy was less than might perhaps have been
expected.   At the same time, the struggle had not gone
far before the name of Origen was dragged in.   He was
denounced by many of the orthodox party as the father
of Arianism, and the Arians were, for the most part,
ready enough to claim his authority for their doctrine
of the Logos.   At the same time there were curious
exceptions to this rule.   Aetius, an Arian writer,
attacked both Origen and Clement, and on the other
side Athanasius defended Origen, and maintained
that the view of the Logos set forth in his writings
was orthodox.   It is true that there were speculations
and suggestions of which Athanasius could not approve,
but his doctrine was in the main sound, and his life
had been that of a holy and wonderful saint.

A few years later, in the middle of the fourth
century, there appears on the scene the little band of
Cappadocian Fathers, Basil of Caesarea, Gregory of

Nazianzus, and Gregory of Nyssa. All three were enthusiastic students of Origen, and the two former edited in his defence the series of extracts from his writings known as the *Philocalia*. It may be of interest to add an account of the teaching of Gregory of Nyssa, in order to illustrate the extent to which the Cappadocians were indebted to their master, and the modifications which the lapse of a century had brought into his system[1]. According to Gregory, Philosophy is not identical with Theology, nor yet on an equality therewith; it rather occupies the position of handmaid. The teaching of Plato can indeed be employed in the defence of Christianity, against polytheism, but there are times when it is necessary for us to leave the Platonic car[2]. He adopts Origen's view that evil is non-being, and he very nearly identifies the principle of evil with matter[3]. God, from Whom all goodness flows, is unchangeable, but the act of creation was itself a change from non-existence into being, and it therefore leaves a possibility of change in its results. On the other hand, Gregory seldom refers to the Neoplatonic distinction between intelligible and sensible, and prefers to make use of the Christian distinctions between Creator and created, Infinite and finite.

In thus attempting to set forth Christian doctrines in a philosophical form, it was inevitable that Gregory should be in some sense the pupil of him who had led the way in this branch of research, and to whom the existing vocabulary of Christian philosophy was

---

[1] Cf. Moore and Wilson, *Nicene and Post-Nicene Fathers*, vol. v.
[2] *De Anim. et Resurr.* Moore and Wilson, p. 8.   [3] *Ib.* p. 9.

due. Hence we are not surprised to find that Gregory adopts and approves of the allegorical method of interpretation. But in other matters we find him introducing changes into his master's system. Thus he combats Origen's theory of the pre-natal existence of the soul[1], accepting the traducianist view, that the world of spirits was created in idea at the beginning, but that each individual soul comes into existence like the body by generation. So too in the case of the resurrection of the body[2]. Gregory partly adopts Origen's teaching, and partly modifies it, and asserts that creation is to be saved by man's carrying his created body into a higher world.

There is then plenty of evidence of the popularity of Origen's writings in the Eastern Church, and of the influence which they exerted. At the same time there was no lack of opposition. Epiphanius, the "sleuth-hound of heresy[3]" was on his track, and made no less than four separate attacks upon his doctrine. His objections fall into three classes, attacks on the alleged Arian tendencies of Origen's teaching, attacks on his psychology, and attacks on the allegorical method of interpretation. But the object of the present section is not so much to give a history of the Origenistic controversies, as to trace out the power and influence of Origen's writings, and therefore we must turn back for a moment, and mark the spread of these doctrines among the Latin-speaking Christians of the West.

The days had long since passed away when

---

[1] Moore and Wilson, p. 19.   [2] *Ib.* p. 21.
[3] Swete, *Patristic Study*, p. 86.

Greek was the natural language in which to address the Christians of Italy, and, although there were of course exceptions, the majority of Western Christians read Greek philosophy and theology only through the medium of Latin translations. Thus it was in Victorinus' translations that Augustine first read the works of the Neoplatonists[1], and in the prefaces to Jerome's commentaries we find references to those Christians who are unable to read Alexandrian theology in the original tongue. Accordingly, at the beginning of the fourth century there was but little real knowledge of Origen in the Western Church, although there was some uneasiness about the views ascribed to him. But in the latter part of this century, two scholars set themselves to translate his works into Latin for the benefit of their fellow-countrymen. These were Jerome and Rufinus, who had gone to Palestine to preside over monasteries at Bethlehem and on the Mount of Olives respectively. Jerome is said by Rufinus to have translated no fewer than seventy of Origen's treatises, and several of his extant works, for instance his *Commentary on the Epistle to the Ephesians*, are largely derived from this source Nor had Jerome, at this early period, any hesitation about defending Origen against his detractors. In a letter to Paula written in 385 A.D.[2], he declares that these attacks are due, not to love of orthodoxy, but to envy of the Alexandrian Father's genius.

But soon there comes a change. In 392 an Egyptian monk named Aterbius visited Jerusalem, and accused Rufinus of heresy, on account of his

---

[1] Aug. *Conf.* 8. 2.   [2] Hieron. *ep.* 33, Migne.

support of Origen. This accusation caused Jerome considerable alarm, and when, two years later, Epiphanius followed with a yet stronger indictment, Jerome declared himself the opponent of Origen's doctrine. Rufinus on the other hand stood firm. He published translations, first of the Apology of Pamphilus and Eusebius, and then of Origen's *De Principiis*, and begged his readers to disregard the cry of heresy, and to learn the truth for themselves. At the same time, he tried to reassure them by declaring his own firm belief in the Holy Trinity and in the resurrection of the body, and by asserting that the heretical passages in Origen's works were later interpolations.

It would be a thankless task to discuss in detail the long and wearisome controversy which followed. Both Jerome and Rufinus allowed themselves to be so far carried away by the heat of the conflict as to forget the moderation which their position as theologians of the Christian Church demanded. The victory rested with the opponents of Origen. Anastasius, Bishop of Rome, after an examination, not indeed of the whole of Origen's works, but of a series of excerpts forwarded to him by the partizans of Epiphanius, formally condemned his writings, and reprimanded Rufinus. The later stages of the quarrel assumed a political rather than a theological character, and need not detain us. But the whole controversy shows the importance of the position which Origen was felt to occupy in Christian speculation, and the interest that was taken in his writings. Even after his condemnation there were probably many like

Theophilus of Alexandria, who continued to read his works "culling the flower and passing by the thorn[1]." Nor must the influence of the Latin translations be forgotten, for even if the works of Rufinus were regarded with disfavour, there was no such stigma attaching to the earlier writings of Jerome, several of which were largely based on Origen.

It is pleasant to turn from the polemics of Epiphanius and Jerome to one of the most delightful characters of the ancient world. Of Synesius the philosopher something has been said in the last chapter : we are now concerned with Synesius the Christian. It is not easy to assign a date to his conversion. He married a Christian lady, perhaps in 403 A.D., and it is probable that three out of his six Christian hymns were written before 406[2]. It is thus reasonable to suppose that he was converted four or five years before his elevation to the Episcopate in 409. But at a yet earlier date, during his visit to Constantinople, we find him ready to pray in the Christian Churches[3], and it is probable that he had scant sympathy with those Neoplatonists who still indulged in theurgy, and opposed Christianity. It has been suggested that his conversion was brought about by two main causes, " a deepening sense of his own difficulty in keeping clean from matter, and a growing sympathy for the needs and sorrows of common people[4]." In other words, he learned by experience the defects of unaided Neoplatonism ; its

---

[1] Socrates, *Hist. Eccl.* 6. 17.
[2] Glover, *Life and Letters in the Fourth Century*, p. 346.
[3] *Hymn.* 3. 448.   [4] Glover, p. 347.

inability to raise man to the high standard which
it set forth, and its lack of a message for any but the
intellectual few.

At the same time Synesius felt no difficulty in
maintaining his philosophical tenets side by side
with the Christian faith. His friendship with Hypatia
was interrupted only by death, and in spite of
the recent controversies, he boldly proclaimed his
Origenistic sympathies before he would permit himself to be consecrated Bishop of Ptolemais. He
refused to give up his belief in the pre-natal existence
of the soul, in the eternity of the world, and in
Origen's doctrine of the resurrection of the body. "If
I can be Bishop on these terms, philosophizing at
home and speaking in parables abroad, I accept the
office....What have the people to do with Philosophy?
Divine truth must be and is rightly an unspeakable
mystery[1]." He adopts in fact the position of Origen,
respecting the claim of the "man in the congregation"
for recognition as a true member of the Church, but
reserving, for himself and those like him, the right
to maintain an esoteric doctrine to which ordinary
persons could not attain. Happily for the people
of Ptolemais, and happily too for the Church,
Theophilus of Alexandria was willing to accept him
on these terms, and to consecrate the man who so
boldly maintained the doctrines which he had himself
elsewhere endeavoured to stamp out.

We must not linger over the history of Synesius'
episcopate. As our knowledge of the man would
lead us to suppose, it was marked by a courageous

[1] Syn. *Ep.* 105; cf. Nicoll, *Synesius*, p. 125.

championship of the poor and suffering, an unflinching
determination to attack and reprove wrong doing in
high places, and a readiness to protect the former
wrong doer when he in turn was threatened with
injustice. Synesius died at some date between 413
and 431, and our knowledge of the Church over
which he presided comes to a close.

vi

It now remains to add some account of the two
writers through whose works the ideas of Neoplatonism
continued to influence men's thought during the
Middle Ages. Both of them were acute thinkers,
strongly influenced by the school of Proclus : one
seems to have been a monk, connected probably with
Edessa, and living at the close of the fifth century ;
the other was one of the most famous scholars and
statesmen of the early decades of the sixth. The
name of the statesman was Boethius, the name of the
monk is unknown, but his works were published
under the pseudonym of 'Dionysius the Areopagite.'
Let us first turn to 'Dionysius[1].' We find the
earliest mention of his writings in 533 A.D. when an
appeal was made to their authority by the Severians,
a monophysite sect at Constantinople. The appeal
was disallowed by the orthodox party on the ground
that a work of the Apostolic age which was unknown
to Cyril and Athanasius was hardly to be considered
authentic. But before many years had elapsed the
writings won their way to wide-spread popularity.

---

[1] See Westcott, *Religious Thought in the West*, pp. 142 ff.

It is true that Photius, in the ninth century, pointed out that the books were unknown to Eusebius and the early Fathers, and that they contained various anachronisms.   But this criticism came too late to interfere with the influence and authority of 'Dionysius.'   For two centuries and a half the books had been quoted with respect by many Greek writers, and in 827 A.D., fifteen or twenty years before the date of Photius' objections, a copy of the writings presented by Michael the Stammerer to Louis I of France had been enshrined with much ceremony in the Abbey of St Denis, where the Areopagite was reputed to have been buried.   From that moment their position in Europe was secure.   Not only did the works of 'Dionysius' exercise a considerable influence upon Joannes Scotus in the ninth century, but from the twelfth to the fifteenth centuries they formed the subject of a whole series of commentaries and translations, written by eminent scholars and ecclesiastics of the day.   It was only after the Renaissance that the doubts about their authenticity were revived, and the Dionysian origin of the books finally disproved.

It was not without reason that the unknown author assumed a title which suggested the combination of Christianity with Greek philosophy.   In the four great treatises which are still extant we find a careful attempt to show that the teaching of Proclus and the teaching of the Church supplement and illuminate each other.   In the first treatise, *On the Heavenly Hierarchy*, 'Dionysius' describes a mighty series or system of creatures, called into existence by God, and together forming an immense ladder of being, stretching down from God's throne. At every stage in this series there is a certain knowledge of God attainable by the faithful worshipper, at every stage too it is possible for him to climb to the stage above, where he will gain a closer fellowship with the Supreme Being[1]. Man is but one link in this mighty chain, and man's view of God is necessarily incomplete. Man is finite and God is infinite, so that man can only speak and think of God in finite and imperfect terms. Yet man's knowledge of God, though incomplete, is not necessarily false, for God reveals Himself to man, alike in the world around us, and by special means which He has employed at various times; and if man makes use of these opportunities, God will lead him on to something higher.

We need not linger over the details of the Heavenly Hierarchy, or follow 'Dionysius' as he traces out the functions of the nine orders of angels. We pass on to the treatise *On the Ecclesiastical Hierarchy*. Here we learn that there is on earth an image or reflection of the great system in the heavens. It stands on a lower level than its heavenly counterpart, just as the material world in which we move is on a lower level than the spiritual world in which the angels have their being[2]. Yet the Church, the Ecclesiastical Hierarchy, is none the less divine in origin, and it has a mighty task entrusted to it. It is the task of bringing salvation to men and to those

[1] Westcott, *R. T. W.* p. 157; Dion. *de Cael Hier.* 1. 3.
[2] *De Eccl. Hier.* 1. 2.

above us,—a salvation that consists in being made like God[1]. The doctrines of the Ecclesiastical Hierarchy have been enshrined in Holy Scriptures, which are themselves inspired by God; its organization, and the sacraments and other services which it employs, symbolize for us various aspects of its fellowship with God. The writer then proceeds to describe in detail various sacraments and ordinances of the Church, adding in every case an explanation of the symbolism.

The object of the third treatise, *On the Divine Names*, is to show that, while we cannot know God entirely as He is, we are yet able, by the right use of our powers and opportunities, to obtain a partial knowledge of Him. We must begin by asserting the Unity of God. God is above all One; all that exists comes from Him, and was therefore itself originally one. And when creation comes to that perfection for which God has designed it, it will be completely at unity with itself and with Him[2]. But while it is easy to assert the Unity of God, it is not possible to comprehend it. For the Unity of the infinite God is beyond all mind, and most of all is it beyond the comprehension of our minds. At the same time there are names which we are right in applying to God, not because they give a complete description of God, but because they are true so far as they go, and describe Him so far as we are able to do so. Some of these names apply to the whole Godhead, for instance Being, Goodness and the like. Others, as Father, Son, Word, Spirit, apply to particular Persons. But both

---

[1] *De Eccl. Hier.* 1. 3.   [2] *De Div. Nom.* 2. 7, 4. 10.

sets of terms are true, and both are inadequate, since they only express God in terms suitable for our limited understandings[1].

The next great characteristic of God, after His Unity, is His Goodness. Just as the sun, because it is the sun, shines on all alike, so God, because He is God, extends His love to all His creatures. There is no corner of creation beyond His reach : there is no creature to which He is not ready to show Himself a loving Father. Or, in other words, "Everything that *is* is from the fair and good, and is in the fair and good, and turns to the fair and good[2]." But if this be so, what are we to say about evil? The answer is that evil, as such, has no real existence. It is a falling short, a failure to reach the full development of which this or that creature was capable. Evil objects exist in abundance, but they owe their existence to the fact that they all partake in some measure, however small, of good. Evil itself is a falling short, and it therefore varies according to the peculiar character of every object in which it is said to occur. It springs from defects of many different kinds, as free beings fail in one way and another to reach the development for which God intended them. "But," says 'Dionysius,' "God knows the evil as it is good[3]." He looks, that is, not at the extent to which this or that being has fallen short of His design, but at the extent to which it is fulfilling it. And it is because to some extent, however small, the evil powers are working for good, that He allows them to continue. In the case of man the matter is further explained

---

[1] *De Div. Nom.* i. i.   [2] Westcott, *R. T. W.* p. 179.
[3] *De Div. Nom.* 4. 30.   Westcott, *R. T. W.* p. 180.

by this, that God has given man freedom of choice, and He respects the free will that He has given. He will not compel man to be good by force.

But a further question arises. If evil has no real existence, and if the sinner is to some extent working out God's purpose, why does God punish him? It is because God gave the sinner power to do a great deal more than he is doing towards carrying His purpose into effect, and He punishes the negligence which the sinner's free choice has caused[1]. 'Dionysius' then goes on to show that all creation is in harmony with God. The purpose for which it was made, and the gradual realisation of that purpose both owe their existence to God, and are derived from Him.

In the last treatise, *On Mystical Theology* 'Dionysius' tries to carry us a little further. He endeavours to enable the reader to rise above the world that we can see and touch and think about, and to secure a truer knowledge of God by laying aside every form of thought or expression which seems to limit Him to the things of this world. In the work *On the Divine Names* the method employed is for the most part affirmative. The writer takes the names which describe God's nature and expounds their meaning. In the present work the negative method naturally predominates, and God is described, not by the attributes which He possesses, but by the limitations from which He is free.

The style of 'Dionysius' is wearisome and verbose, and it is easy to quote phrases and paragraphs which appear to the modern reader to be meaningless jargon. But the foregoing summary will suffice to

[1] *De Div. Nom.* 4. 35.

show that 'Dionysius' made a real contribution to
human thought, and that apart from the title which
he assumed, his works contained a living message for
those who could understand them.

The personal history of 'Dionysius' can only be
pieced together from the internal evidence of his
writings. With Boethius however the case is different[1].
His father, Aurelius Manlius Boethius, held various
important posts under Odovacar, rising to the consulship in 487 A.D. Anicius Manlius Severinus Boethius
was born in or about the year 480, and though he
was yet a mere child when his father died, he was
carefully educated by his kinsmen Festus and
Symmachus. He learned Greek and was soon
attracted by Greek works on science and philosophy of
all kinds, many of which he translated for the benefit
of his Latin-speaking contemporaries. He also wrote
several commentaries on the works of Aristotle, and
composed a series of *Theological Tracts* in which he
attempted to apply philosophical methods to the current
doctrinal controversies. Boethius must have become
acquainted with Theodoric soon after that Emperor's
arrival in Rome in the year 504: for we find him elected
Sole Consul in 510, and he enjoyed the Emperor's
favour long enough to see his two sons elevated to
the Consulship in 522. But suddenly his fortune
changed. An injudicious speech in praise of old
Roman freedom awakened Theodoric's suspicions:
Boethius was arraigned and imprisoned, and after being
condemned by the Senate he was tortured and put
to death with a club.

[1] Cf. H. F. Stewart, *Boethius*.

During his imprisonment he wrote five books *On the Consolation of Philosophy*. In the first book he describes himself in the prison, weeping and striving in vain to distract his thoughts by writing verses. Suddenly there appears before him the stately figure of Philosophy. She is a woman, venerable in appearance yet ever young, clad in a robe of her own weaving, holding a book in one hand and a sceptre in the other. She drives away the Muses, and stays herself to comfort the prisoner. In the remainder of the work Boethius tells how his mysterious visitor reasoned with him, brushing aside his anger against Fortune, who is a true friend only when she frowns: showing how insufficient are the aims which most men seek to achieve, and pointing out that while the triumph of the wicked in the world is always more apparent than real, their punishment is swift and inevitable. This leads on to a discussion about the difference between Providence and Fate, and the relation of both to the divine Simplicity: and the work closes with an elaborate discussion of man's free will, as it exists side by side with the fore-knowledge of God.

It is remarkable that in this work the leading ideas of Christianity should be almost entirely omitted. There is no reason to suppose that Boethius was a heathen. The *Theological Tracts* show clearly enough that he was well acquainted with western theology ; and yet in the books with which he solaced the dreariness of his imprisonment there is no word about a Redeemer. The standpoint from which he writes is throughout that of the Neoplatonist, and the

references to Christianity are few and far between.
Are we to suppose that Boethius had given up
all faith in the Gospel and turned instead to the
consolations of Philosophy? Yet if that were so we
should expect to find some expression of disappoint-
ment or bitterness against the support that had failed
him. Another explanation has however been suggested[1]. The style of the treatise is throughout cold
and formal, and it may be that it was written, like the
verses which Boethius was composing when Philosophy
appeared, merely to while away the tedious hours of
confinement. If this be so, we should be mistaken
in regarding the work as the expression of Boethius'
ultimate grounds of confidence, and must look on it
rather as a task undertaken in order to distract his
attention during a time of suspense. If this theory
be accepted, the treatise loses somewhat in reality,
but we have at the same time a key to a problem
which might otherwise be difficult to solve.

The popularity of Boethius in the Middle Ages
was extraordinary[2]. It would be difficult to find a
secular writer whose works were more often translated
or more widely read. In our own land his influence
is to be traced in *Beowulf*, the earliest of Anglo-
Saxon epics (c. 800 A.D.), whilst the *Consolation of
Philosophy* was translated or paraphrased by King
Alfred (878), and in later days by Chaucer (1340–
1400). Nor were other countries less willing to do
him honour. Between the eleventh and the fourteenth
centuries translations of the *Consolation* were published
in France, Italy, Germany, Spain and Greece, and

[1] Stewart, p. 106.　　　　[2] See Stewart, *Boethius*, c. VI.

indirect references are to be found in many poems and romances as well. The fame and influence of 'Dionysius' and of Boethius alike, have long since died away. There are few persons of ordinary culture to-day who could if asked either tell the names or describe the contents of their writings. Nor is the reason difficult to find. They transmitted to the Middle Ages something of the spirit of Greek philosophy, and in so doing they conferred a great and lasting benefit. But when in the fifteenth century learning revived, and men began once more to study the Greek classics for themselves, the lustre of 'Dionysius' and Boethius was bound to wane. They had done their work, and when the literature from which their inspiration was derived came to be widely known and read, they relapsed into comparative obscurity.

It is impossible, within the bounds of this essay, to trace the influence of Neoplatonism upon mediaeval and modern thought. The speculations of Joannes Scotus, and their reception by the theologians of his time, the rise of the Cambridge Platonists in the seventeenth century, the attention that is paid to-day, alike to Plotinus and his school, and to the Christian Fathers who in part reflect their teaching, show clearly that the force of Neoplatonism did not perish when Justinian closed the lecture-rooms. But these themes, attractive and fascinating as they are, would carry us far beyond the limits of the present work.

Two questions however remain upon which a few words may be added. What caused the failure of Neoplatonism to hold its own against the spread of Christianity, and what was the contribution that it made to the development of Christian theology? To the first of these questions the answer would seem to be, that Neoplatonism even in its highest and purest form, was incapable of answering all the questions which man seeks to solve. It dealt exclusively with abstract Principles. It spoke of a supreme Being, but never of a personal God. It told of beauty and goodness, but never of love. And therefore it failed to claim the allegiance of the whole man. It was in fact throughout an intellectual system, and it could never satisfy the cravings of the human heart.

But, with regard to the second question, it would be a mistake to suppose that Neoplatonism made no contribution to Christian theology. "In divers portions and in divers manners," God spake "in time past to the fathers in the prophets[1]." Little by little, as man was able to receive it, the message was given. And, though the revelation was completed once and for all, in the coming of our Lord Jesus Christ, it was still necessary for its content to be worked out and assimilated. And Neoplatonism, under the guiding hand of God, helped to bring out some aspects of the truth which might otherwise have long remained unnoticed. The earliest Christians, trained under the strict discipline of the Jewish law, had received definite teaching about the unity and the eternal existence of God. They knew that the world was made by

[1] Heb. i. 1.

Him, and that it is not co-extensive with Him. They knew also that He is not the author of evil, and that the evil in the world is not destined to be eternal. But soon the Gospel spread to men and races unfamiliar with these doctrines, and there was a danger that they would be allowed to lapse. It was the task of the Neoplatonists, through the Christians who came under their influence, once more to draw men's attention to such truths as these, and to prevent them from falling into oblivion. This was its work in the third and fourth centuries, when so many of the doctrines of Christian theology were taking definite shape. And its reappearance from time to time in the ages that have followed has served as a witness that the eternal verities are still beyond human comprehension. It reminds us that our theology should be a living organism, that we must not be contented merely to repeat the formulae of an earlier age, but strive constantly after fuller knowledge and closer fellowship with the Divine.

INDEX

For EU product safety concerns, contact us at Calle de José Abascal, 56–1°, 28003 Madrid, Spain or eugpsr@cambridge.org.

www.ingramcontent.com/pod-product-compliance
Ingram Content Group UK Ltd.
Pitfield, Milton Keynes, MK11 3LW, UK
UKHW012332130625
459647UK00009B/237